Marketing Case Studies

The Marketing Series is one of the most comprehensive collections of books in marketing and sales available from the UK today.

Published by Butterworth-Heinemann on behalf of The Chartered Institute of Marketing, the series is divided into three distinct groups: *Student* (fulfilling the needs of those taking the Institute's certificate and diploma qualifications); *Professional Development* (for those on formal or self-study vocational training programmes); and *Practitioner* (presented in a more informal, motivating and highly practical manner for the busy marketer).

Formed in 1911, The Chartered Institute of Marketing is now the largest professional marketing management body in Europe with over 24 000 members and 28 000 students located worldwide. Its primary objectives are focused on the development of awareness and understanding of marketing throughout UK industry and commerce and in the raising of standards of professionalism in the education, training and practice of this key business discipline.

Titles in the series

Business Law
R. G. Lawson and D. Smith

Cases in Marketing Financial Services
Edited by Chris Ennew, Trevor Watkins and Mike Wright

Consumer Behaviour
Chris Rice

Economic Theory and Marketing Practice
Angela Hatton and Mike Oldroyd

Effective Sales Management
John Strafford and Colin Grant

Financial Aspects of Marketing
Keith Ward

The Fundamentals of Advertising
John Wilmshurst

The Fundamentals and Practice of Marketing
John Wilmshurst

International Marketing
Stanley J. Paliwoda

Marketing Communications
C. L. Coulson-Thomas

Marketing Financial Services
Edited by Chris Ennew, Trevor Watkins and Mike Wright

Marketing Case Studies
Lester Massingham and Geoff Lancaster

The Principles and Practice of Selling
A. Gillam

Strategic Marketing Management
R. M. S. Wilson and C. T. Gilligan with D. Pearson

Marketing Case Studies

How to tackle them:
How to answer them

Second edition

LESTER MASSINGHAM AND GEOFF LANCASTER

Published on behalf of
The Chartered Institute of Marketing

Butterworth-Heinemann Ltd
Linacre House, Jordan Hill, Oxford OX2 8DP

℞ A member of the Reed Elsevier plc group

OXFORD   LONDON   BOSTON
MUNICH   NEW DELHI   SINGAPORE   SYDNEY
TOKYO   TORONTO   WELLINGTON

First published as *Mini Cases in Marketing* 1990
Reprinted 1991, 1992
Second edition 1995

© Lester Massingham and Geoff Lancaster 1990, 1995

British Library Cataloguing in Publication Data
A catalogue record for this book is available from the
British Library

ISBN 0 7506 2011 0

Printed in Great Britain by Clays, St Ives plc

Contents

Acknowledgements

Our thanks to the senior examiners of The Chartered Institute of Marketing (CIM) and to Norman Waite, Director of Education, and Doyne North, Education Manager of the CIM, for permission to reproduce case studies that have previously featured in CIM examinations.

We also thank Pam Mathews of Marketing Education Consultants for the assistance provided in preparing this manuscript.

Part One   How to Pass the Mini-case

1 *Introduction*

1.1 The need for this text

In 1990 the authors of this text, together with the publishers, Butterworth-Heinemann, launched a text written specifically to help students of marketing tackle 'mini-case studies'. This form of examining was becoming at that time, and still is, increasingly popular for examining marketing in first degree and diploma courses and many higher degree courses.

Such examining was pioneered by The Chartered Institute of Marketing (CIM) when it introduced the mini-case concept – first into its final diploma subjects and then into the certificate level subjects, Practice of sales management and Practice of marketing.

In its first edition, therefore, this book was intended to provide students with a step-by-step guide to tackling mini-cases and in particular to help in the preparation for the new CIM examinations which used this format.

The mini-case format has proved to be so successful and popular that, as hinted earlier, its use has been increasingly adopted by examiners and examining bodies in marketing. In fact, the CIM in their new 'Syllabus 94' syllabuses and examinations have taken the opportunity not only to retain the mini-case type format but also to both refine and extend the use of this very practical type of examination.

With the introduction of the Syllabus 94 initiative the CIM determined that in the future, with the exception of the diploma level Analysis and Decision paper, which is to retain its maxi-case format, *all* examination papers will now have two parts. The two parts will consist of a compulsory Part A, and a Part B offering a choice of questions. It is the compulsory Part A which will have questions based on either a mini-case or sometimes, at Certificate and Advanced Certificate level, some 'stimulus' material such as a press cutting or a quote from an academic journal.

Notwithstanding the possible use of such stimulus material as a basis of marketing scenarios, therefore, the mini-case is here to stay.

The situation now is that the mini-case will remain in the format used in Part A of three of the Diploma level subjects as follows:

- Marketing Communications Strategy
- International Marketing Strategy
- Planning and Control.

At the Advanced Certificate level mini-cases will also figure strongly, though occasionally the sort of stimulus material referred to earlier will also be used. This means that the mini-case format can and will be used in the following subjects:

- Promotional Practice
- Management Information for Marketing and Sales
- Effective Management for Marketing
- Effective Management for Sales
- Marketing Operations
- Sales Operations.

At the Certificate level, more use will be made of the stimulus-type material than at the successive Advanced Certificate and Diploma levels. However, even here a mini-case type format may also be used. We have used the term mini-case 'type' because at this level any cases will be very brief indeed. At the risk of confusing the issue we could even call them 'mini'-mini-cases. Because they are likely to be so brief, as compared with the already brief mini-cases used at Advanced Certificate and Diploma level, the approach required is somewhat different to that appropriate to the conventional mini-case and primarily discussed in this text. However, there are also some similarities in that, even at Certificate level, the examiners are testing practical application skills often requiring memo- or report-type formats based on actual or hypothetical marketing problems. Because of this, although perhaps not true mini-cases as such, we have included samples of these mini-mini-cases from some of the Certificate level subjects. In the main, however, we have focused on the more conventional mini-case formats as pioneered in the Diploma subjects.

As in the first edition of this text, as you may already have gleaned, although the techniques and skills discussed are relevant to any mini-case the text is primarily aimed at students preparing for the examinations of The Chartered Institute of Marketing. Great reliance has therefore been placed upon actual cases and specimen answers.

1.2 The structure of the text

You will find that the text is divided into ten main parts. Part One focuses on the mini-case structure and how to approach this type of examination format. Essentially this part of the text is aimed at explaining how to tackle a mini-case and hence increase your chances of passing.

In Chapter 2 we start by familiarizing you with the 'typical' structure and format of the mini-cases, noting the most important points about the format of these cases when you come to attempt them. We also highlight the important differences between the intentionally short mini-case format and the extended case format such as that used by the CIM for the Analysis and Decision case at Diploma level. In addition to explaining the format and differences associated with mini-cases we shall also be explaining the sort of questions to expect on the mini-cases, and what the examiners are typically looking for in their marking. In this chapter we introduce our first example of an actual mini-case.

Having familiarized you with these aspects, in Chapter 3 we then move on to explain a framework for tackling mini-cases, together with some further considerations in preparing your answers. At this stage we are ready to begin to detail the analysis of mini-cases. Wherever possible in the text we have used actual mini-cases for our sample/practice cases. Clearly this helps to ensure that the cases you encounter in this text will be similar to those you can expect in the CIM examinations.

In addition to helping reinforce our points about format and the types of questions which you can expect, we have used the first three sample mini-cases to illustrate some of the most important points to be aware of when analysing the mini-case and answering the set questions. You will see that in order to do this we have used a system of annotating the sample cases and questions in order to highlight the key points.

In addition, for each of these first three sample cases, we have also included a detailed analysis of the examiners' comments in order to illustrate some of the more common mistakes made by mini-case candidates in the past. By doing this we hope, of course, to reduce the chances that you will make the same mistakes.

In Chapter 4, we concentrate on a selection of worked examples of mini-cases. Here we illustrate how all the skills, techniques and frameworks outlined in earlier chapters come together when faced with a mini-case. A selection of mini-cases from both Certificate and Diploma level subjects has been used by way of example in this section so as to be relevant to as many potential candidates as possible.

Chapter 5 is the penultimate chapter of Part One, and here we offer guidance on how to structure your answers. In particular we look at the techniques of report writing. Finally, Chapter 6 highlights some of the most common causes of failure on the mini-cases and discusses how to minimize these.

In Part Two of the text the onus is very much on you. A series of mini-cases is provided covering the range of subjects on the CIM's new Syllabus 94 examinations where mini-cases might be used. For ease of reference these have been organized by stage: Chapter 8 includes a selection of Certificate and Advanced Certificate mini-cases, and Chapter 9 mini-cases for the Diploma stage subjects. These are for you to practise on under self-imposed examination conditions in the manner outlined in 1.3 below. Specimen answers for each of the cases are contained in Chapters 10 and 11 for the Certificate subjects and Chapter 11 for the Diploma.

These cases have been carefully selected to provide a good indication of the range of formats and styles which you might expect to encounter in the examinations which you are taking. Clearly you will need to select the chapters which pertain to the stage that you are studying for.

1.3 How to use this book

Using the approach and techniques which you have learned about in Part One of the text, you should systematically work through the relevant specimen cases in your own time.

In order to get the most out of your work on these cases it is important
that you follow the following instructions with regard to procedure:

- Treat each mini-case as a mock examination. Specifically:
  - Time yourself. Try to spend only the amount of time on each specimen
    case which you would have in the actual examination.
  - Don't use any notes or textbooks.
  - Try to ensure that you are not interrupted.
  - Don't be tempted to 'skim through' the specimen cases before you are
    ready to tackle them as 'examination' cases.
  - Most important of all, don't look at the specimen answers to the cases
    which we have included in subsequent chapters (see below).
- Compare your finished answer with the specimen answers included in
  subsequent chapters.

When you have completed your first specimen mini-cases then, and only
then, can you turn to the respective specimen answer chapters. For each of
these specimen cases we have given a suggested answer so that you can
evaluate how your answer compares with an 'expert' answer. Don't worry if
your answer is not the same as the specimen answer, especially as regards
recommendations. It is important to learn that there is no one 'right' answer
to a case study. However, we (and the examiners) would have expected you
to identify and agree the key issues in the cases, and your overall approach
should be broadly similar to that shown in the suggested answers.

We can now move on to discuss what to expect in the mini-case studies.

2 The mini-case studies: what to expect

2.1 Background

As mentioned earlier, the CIM was foremost in the introduction and use of the mini-case format in Marketing examinations.

In addition as we have also mentioned, the success of the mini-case is helping to meet the Institute's aims of developing professional competent marketers and has prompted an extension of their use in every level of the Syllabus 94 examining process.

Before the introduction of the mini-case format, most of the subjects for the CIM examinations were mainly examined through traditional essay-type questions where candidates were required to demonstrate their knowledge and understanding of concepts and techniques rather than an ability to apply such knowledge in a practical context.

Quite rightly, however, the Institute recognized that its qualification is, in a very real sense, a licence to practise, and because of this, in addition to testing knowledge and understanding of concepts the Institute needed to encourage and assess through their examinations the necessary managerial skills of future professional marketers. The mini-case format is ideal for these purposes and in particular seeks to assess the following skills/competences:

- Analytical skills
- Skills of working under time pressure and with incomplete information
- Decision-making skills
- Application skills
- Management communication skills.

Marketing is not just an academic discipline; it is primarily a management function. As such, anyone claiming to be a skilled marketing professional must be able to demonstrate that they can apply their skills and knowledge to 'real life' marketing procedures. The Institute's examiners will be using a variety of formats to test these skills in current and future examinations, including press clippings, seminars, etc. However, the principal format used will be that of the mini-case, and it is to this format that we now turn our attention.

2.2 The format and style of the mini-cases

The first thing to recognize about the format and style of the mini-cases in the CIM examination is that both may vary. Both the length and the style of the mini-cases used will, perhaps understandably, vary a little both between the different subjects and over time. Indeed, one of the things you will become familiar with from studying and working on the cases in this text is the variety of styles used in the mini-cases.

2.2.1 Content of the mini-cases

Obviously the content of the mini-cases is different for each subject and each examination. Bearing this in mind, it is possible to generalize about what you can expect with regard to format and style as follows. Sometimes the mini-case will be focused on a set of quite specific marketing problems within a particular organization. Sometimes it will be more general in nature and require the candidate to identify the major marketing issues in the case, albeit based on the specific questions asked by the examiner. Sometimes it will not really be a case at all; rather, it will be more of an outline of a given business situation or a scenario. However, for the most part the overall framework for dealing with mini-cases outlined later in Chapter 4 can still be used, and in fact we have included some of these business situations or 'scenario-type' cases for you to learn from.

Finally, you will find that at both the Certificate and Advanced Certificate levels an article or press cutting will be used instead of a mini-case. Like the mini-case, the use of these articles and press cuttings is intended to test skills of application in specified contexts. Essentially the use of mini-case techniques is still appropriate where this type of examination format is used, and this format is included in the sample cases in the text.

Of necessity, the information contained in the mini-cases tends to be much more focused according to the particular subject of each examination than that found in, say, the open-book maxi-case study for analysis and decision. This and other differences between the mini- and maxi-case formats and contents are important and are therefore explored in more depth later in this chapter.

2.2.2 Sectionalization of paper/instructions to candidates

With the exception of the analysis and decision (maxi-case) paper, all of the examination papers for Certificate, Advanced Certificate and Diploma level subjects are comprised of two parts, A and B. The mini-cases are used only in Part A, with Part B usually being comprised of more traditional essay-type/discussion questions.

Part A is compulsory for all papers, which clearly heightens the importance of good mini-case technique. At the moment Part A normally constitutes the percentage of marks shown below:

Certificate level subjects: 40 per cent of marks
Advanced Certificate level subjects: 50 per cent of marks
Diploma level subjects: 50 per cent of marks.

In any event, as we shall see, the CIM ensures that every examination paper contains clear instructions and information for candidates about the mark allocation to each Part. Obviously it is vital that you read and follow these carefully whenever you present yourself for one of the Institute's examinations. One of the most important implications of paying heed to the mark allocation for each Part of the paper is that it enables you to plan your time allocation. Clearly, if the mini-case in Part A is worth 40 per cent of the marks on a three-hour paper (which all of the Institute's papers are), you will need to allocate your time accordingly, i.e. approximately $1\frac{1}{4}$ hours for Part A. Similarly, where Part A is worth 50 per cent of the marks you should allocate approximately $1\frac{1}{2}$ hours to this Part.

2.2.3 *Number of questions on the mini-case and mark allocations to questions*

Often the mini-case in Part A will require you to answer more than one question. Where there is more than one question and/or where the questions are comprised of subsections, normally the mark allocation to each question/ subsection will be shown. You will see from the cases included in this text that the precise question format for the mini-cases and, indeed, the number of questions you may be asked may vary between subjects and from year to year.
   Sometimes in the instructions to candidates with the mini-cases you will be asked to play a particular role when answering the questions on the case, e.g. 'acting as marketing consultant', or 'you are the newly appointed marketing manager for the company'. Clearly, if you are asked to play such a role you should tackle your answers from this perspective.

2.2.4 *Answer format for mini-cases*

An essay-type format is inappropriate for answering mini-case questions. Often the precise format required in an answer will be specified in the question itself, with report- and/or memorandum-type formats being particularly favoured. Clearly, you should again follow the instructions closely as to the required format for the answer. Owing to the prevalence of report-memo-type formats in the mini-cases these are explained in greater detail later in the text.
   Now we need to expand on the differences between short mini-cases and the extended maxi-case such as that used by the CIM for the Diploma Analysis and Research examination.

2.3 Differences between mini-cases and the maxi-case (analysis and decision)

If mini-cases were exactly the same as the extended maxi-case study, there would really be no point in having them. The most obvious difference is in terms of length of mini-cases compared with the analysis and decision case, together with the amount of information you have to work upon. In addition, there are a number of other important distinctions between these short cases and the maxi-case.

1 The mini-case examination is unseen. Unlike the analysis and decision case, you will only be presented with the actual mini-case in the examination itself. This, of course, means that you have very little time in which to ascertain the most relevant details. In reality, the issues tend to be far less complex, and it must be remembered that all candidates are similarly disadvantaged.

2 Because these cases are so much shorter than the analysis and decision cases you will not be expected, nor, indeed, will it be possible, to prepare sophisticated and extended analyses for these mini-cases. The maxi-case, on the other hand, often contains data which are not strictly relevant to the problems set because this type of case is usually based upon a factual situation – some of which is relevant and some irrelevant. It is normally the situation when preparing a mini-case that the questions are set at the same time as the case material is prepared, so it is more likely that these questions will relate specifically to the case.

3 At all levels of the CIM examinations, the emphasis in the case studies is on practical/application skills. The extended Analysis and Decision case study, however, does inevitably require much more time to be spent on analysis and, indeed, contains substantial data on which such extended analysis can be based.

4 A final point is not so much an absolute difference between mini-cases and the analysis and decision case, but is more one of emphasis. A feature of past CIM mini-cases is that a significant proportion feature small and sometimes relatively inexperienced companies, inexperienced would-be exporters, small businesses with a sole principal and so on. This is not to say that this will always be the situation.

As marketing applications develop and expand, and as changes take root, the CIM, through its examiners, may wish to test your knowledge and awareness of these changes and their implications with regard to marketing practice. For example, in the public sector, increasing attention is being paid to the marketing of services and the application of marketing principles and practice to the non-profit-making and public sectors.

Similarly, there is now much more interest in aspects such as consumerism, green issues and social responsibility in marketing. The mini-case format represents an ideal vehicle for testing a candidate's knowledge of such contemporary and topical trends and events in marketing. Thus you can now expect to see these aspects being tested in the mini-cases.

2.4 Summary of learning points

1 The CIM's mini-cases are specifically designed to test your skills in application rather than your ability to write academic-type essays.
2 As in business, effective time allocation is essential. The proportion of total marks accounted for by each question provides a clue as to what this should be. Where no indication is given, it is reasonably safe to assume that all questions are accorded equal marks.
3 Beware of making your analysis of the mini-case your full answer unless, of course, the questions specifically ask you to do this. In other words, only answer what the question requires you to answer.
4 Do not waste time on extended general introductions which are designed merely to analyse the existing position; this will only waste valuable time and not earn marks. It is so easy to overrun time when answering the mini-case questions.
5 Ensure that you adopt the correct format for your answers. Normally this will be report- or memo-type format.

2.5 A sample mini-case

It is perhaps difficult to begin to appreciate many of the points we have covered so far if you have never seen an actual mini-case. To conclude this chapter, therefore, it is appropriate, for those in this position, to introduce our first sample mini-case which is reproduced below.

We have used the Advanced Certificate Level Marketing Operations paper by way of example, but do not worry if you are not actually taking this subject. The general approach is, of course, similar for all subjects. So that you can get a feel for the structure and content of the examinations we have included not only the Part A mini-case but the full paper, including the rubric and instructions and the essay-type questions in Part B. If you have not seen a mini-case paper before (and perhaps even if you have) you should spend time familiarizing yourself with this 'typical' paper. We suggest that you read through the paper at least twice, noting the instructions to candidates, the mark allocations to each subsection and the general style used in the paper.

Even if you are studying this subject at this stage, do not attempt to analyse the mini-case or put forward your solutions. You will have plenty of opportunity for developing and practising these skills later; here, simply start to get used to the structure. We shall then move on in Chapter 3 to providing a framework for tackling the mini-cases.

A sample mini-case

The Chartered Institute of Marketing

Advanced Certificate In Marketing

Marketing Operations   **Time: 14.00–17.00**

Date: Thursday 8th December 1994   **3 Hours Duration**

SYLLABUS 94

This examination is in two sections.

Part A is compulsory and worth 50% of total marks.

Part B has five questions, select two. Each answer will be worth 25% of the total marks.

DO NOT repeat the question in your answer but show clearly the number of the question attempted on appropriate pages of the answer book.

Rough workings should be included in the answer book and ruled through after use.

Part A
Computer games for all

For millions of children world-wide, computer games have become an established part of growing up. For companies wishing to stay ahead in this industry, the emphasis is on rapid and continual technological innovation. This is a market where product life cycles are short and competitive edge is linked to producing new ideas. Dominant players Nintendo and Sega have managed to achieve the required innovativeness and world-wide are estimated to hold a 90 per cent stake of the hugely profitable £9 billion video game market. The two players compete aggressively for market share with an intensity which has been likened to Coca Cola and Pepsi, Nike and Reebok, and McDonald's and Burger King. Both companies protect their positions through global licensing agreements which ensure control over the distribution of the two brands.

In the UK, recent volume share figures indicate that in certain market sectors Sega has edged ahead of Nintendo. World-wide, at the beginning of 1993, Nintendo was maintaining its lead over Sega. However, both companies realize that current high profit margins will not last forever. Already, a situation of near saturation has been reached in the key US and Japanese markets, switching the attention firmly towards European markets. Like the US and Japan, the European markets will also become saturated and sales growth will slow. This will be a testing time for Nintendo and Sega. The arch rivals will need to pay careful attention to brand building to maintain their shares. Sega has deliberately centred its entire positioning strategy on its brand name in the hope that as the technology gap between alternative manufacturers' games narrows, consumers will perceive the brand name as a product benefit in its own right. The companies are also having to cope with adverse publicity relating to high pricing in certain markets. In the UK Nintendo and Sega have been referred to the Monopolies and Mergers Commission which will review the strict licensing agreements and the 30 per cent price premium charged for games in the UK compared with the US.

As the market matures and sales stabilize, both Nintendo and Sega have focused attention on new promotional ideas – the possibilities for pan-European marketing strategies have received particular attention. Meanwhile Nintendo has taken steps to spread its risk by reducing its reliance on the children's market. Early in the 1990s, the company announced a series of adult-orientated advertisements, called 'Never Get Old' and aimed at people between the ages of 18 and 40, to promote a new software series called InfoGenius. The intention was to capitalize on company research which indicated that some 40 per cent of Game Boy buyers were over the age of 18. Company executives therefore decided to market this enormously popular system as an adult way to have fun.

Although key industry players strongly believe that computer games are not a fad and will retain their popularity over time, efforts are needed to ensure that this type of play becomes established as an integral part of family life, it seems likely that in the future home entertainment will be increasingly

Marketing Case Studies

centred on the television, with crossovers between computer games, sound systems and camcorders. To stay ahead, Sega and Nintendo will need to build on co-operative deals with entertainment providers in the music and film industries such as those which have already resulted in a film version of Nintendo's Super Mario Brothers and cartoon of Sega's Sonic the Hedgehog.

Question 1

In the role of a marketing advisor, write a business report covering the following aspects:

(a) The case suggests that opportunities are likely to arise for crossovers or joint ventures with other forms of home entertainment. Assume that Nintendo is considering liaising with partners from the electronics industry and music business to develop an integrated home entertainment system. Nintendo decides to conduct a marketing audit to provide input into the marketing planning process. Explain the categories of information which should be collected. **(25 marks)**

(b) What legal, regulatory, ethical or social responsibility constraints might Nintendo have to consider before making marketing decisions?

(15 marks)

(c) What do you think are the main opportunities arising from the co-operative deals in which Nintendo might become involved? **(10 marks)**

Part B – Answer TWO questions only

Question 2

You have applied for a job as trainee marketing manager for a large multinational company of your choice. Having successfully passed the first interview, the next stage of the selection involves preparing a brief report which discusses how variables from the marketing environment might affect the company's marketing programmes.

Make sure that your report covers all elements of the marketing environment, suggesting those which you think might be the most important in the selected market and what impact they might have.

Question 3

You work in the publicity department of fast-food retailer Yummy Burger Ltd. Below is an extract from a local newspaper which has been running a series of articles examining the need for more environmentally friendly products and packaging.

'Despite national concern about global warming and the fragile state of the environment, local fast-food retailer Yummy Burger Ltd. continues to use large quantities of non-biodegradable packaging. The few litter bins that are provided are emptied so infrequently that local people continually have rubbish blowing through their gardens. According to local resident Mr Green: 'It's disgusting. Before I leave for work each day I spend 10 minutes picking up Yummy Burger packaging. My rubbish bins are full of it!'

Senior Yummy Burger management has been surprised by the bad publicity and is concerned to minimize future problems of this kind. Members of the board have asked you to make a presentation to them which defines ethics and social responsibility, explains how these issues might impact upon the business and discusses how the company can be better prepared to handle them in the future. Draft a document which discusses the areas you intend to cover in the presentation.

Question 4

As a market researcher who specializes in the car industry, you feel that now would be a good time to review how the industry segments its market. You intend to conduct an extensive information gathering exercise to determine how key players in the industry use market segmentation and what benefits they receive from so doing. In order to carry out your research you need to attract funds and believe that some of the car manufacturers may be interested in becoming involved.

Prepare a proposal aimed at attracting funds from car manufacturers. The proposal should explain what market segmentation is, give details of its benefits and describe some of the base variables which might be appropriate in the car market.

Question 5

Marketing experts sometimes claim that industrial (business-to-business) markets have particular characteristics which make them different to other types of markets. These experts also claim that companies must be aware of these characteristics in their marketing operations.

Assume the role of a marketing consultant who has been asked to explain the effects which the characteristics of industrial markets have on marketing operations. You should centre your explanation around an industry example of your choice.

Question 6

You are managing director of a successful medium sized company producing handmade wooden toys. Following the removal of trade barriers in Europe, you decide that you would like to start trading away from your traditional home market. In order to do this you will need to employ a number of marketing personnel, but are unsure about how to organize the marketing operation away from the UK.

What options do you have for organizing marketing activities in the UK and away from your home market, for example, by function or product or region or customer type? What would be the most appropriate way for your company to begin its exporting activities (for example, exporting, licensing, joint ventures) and why?

3 Tackling mini-cases

3.1 An overall framework

We have seen that one of the key differences between the mini-cases and the extended Analysis and Decision case is the fact that the mini-case is unseen, so the first time you will see the mini-case for each of the three subjects in which this format is used will be in the examination itself. A further key difference which we have seen, and which also has an important bearing on how you tackle the mini-case, is the fact that you are given the questions at the same time as the case. The final key difference for tackling the mini-case is that you have *only* $1\frac{1}{4}$–$1\frac{1}{2}$ *hours* to complete the task.

Bearing these differences in mind, here is a suggested framework for dealing with the mini-case.

Familiarization with case and questions
Analysis of questions/ instructions
Analysis of case material in relation to questions set
Preparation of answers to questions using appropriate format

3.2 Using this format

3.2.1 Stage 1: Familiarization with case and questions

Read through the case and questions quickly a couple of times to familiarize yourself with the case and question scenario. At this stage you should avoid the strong temptation to start writing answers or suggesting detailed solutions to the problems which you spot. At this stage you are simply getting the 'feel' of what the situation and company is 'about', set against the context of the questions/requirements posed by the examiner.

3.2.2 Stage 2: Analysis of questions/instructions

Now turn your attention to the specific questions/instructions which will accompany the mini-cases. It is most important that you follow these to the letter. It may appear strange to have to stress this obvious point, but as we shall see it is still a major point of criticism of candidates by the examiners. For example, if the question asks you to advise on a promotional plan do not subsequently advise on a plan for the marketing mix.

In particular at this stage you should note any instructions as to the *role* you are to assume. For example:

Are you to be a member of the organization?

If so, in what capacity?

Alternatively, for example, you might be asked to assume the role of outside adviser/consultant to the company in the case.

Whatever the role, you should be careful to assume the appropriate stance.

• Remember, in analysing the questions/instructions you should carefully note the mark allocation for each section which should guide you as to the relative importance, and therefore the amount of time, you should devote to each part of your answer.

3.2.3 Stage 3: Analysis of case material in relation to questions set

Now, and only now, are you in a position to work through the case material in detail. Bearing in mind the tasks set for you by the examiner, you should work through the case noting and writing down your *general observations* and any *salient* facts.

Remember, this is your analysis in preparing for your answers, *not the answers themselves*. You should, therefore, prepare this outline in rough and cross it out afterwards. In other words, unless specifically required to do so do not include it as part of your answers. It is for your purposes, not the examiner's.

Again, because of the differences between the mini-cases and the maxi-case of Analysis and Decision, it is unlikely that you will be required, or able to prepare, say, a *detailed* SWOT analysis or a *full* marketing audit. However, so far as it is possible, there is nothing wrong with using these in the context of *analysing* a mini-case, so long as you do not simply rewrite the case under these headings. Overall, your observations of facts and issues should be concise and tailored to the questions themselves.

3.2.4 Stage 4: Preparation of specific answers to questions set

You should now be in a position to turn your attention to producing specific answers to the questions set. Clearly, the content of your answers will need to reflect the particular questions on each case, but remember that the mini-cases are designed to test your *application skills.* You will, therefore, need to select from your acquired knowledge those techniques. concepts and skills which are appropriate to the questions asked.

In preparing your answers you should bear these points in mind:

- *Avoid 'waffle' and extended general introductions.*
  Remember, you have little time to answer the questions set. More importantly, there are *no marks* for general situation analyses or for observations *not directly related to the questions.* In particular, do not waste valuable time by writing down the questions again.
- *Note carefully any constraints and time scales.*
  One of the most frequent criticisms aimed at mini-case answers by the senior examiners is that the candidate has come up with impractical suggestions. As we have noted, very often the mini-cases deal with the marketing problems of smaller or inexperienced companies. A company with an annual turnover of, say, £1 to £2 million is unlikely to be able to afford, for example, a national television advertising campaign or, say, an extensive and expensive programme of international marketing research. The recognition of the limiting effects of such resource constraints – financial, human and organizational – and a reflection of these in your answers is yet another variation on the test of your ability to practise marketing. Sometimes the cases themselves will contain specific information on budgets, e.g. for promotion. Do not exceed them; demonstrate your professional knowledge of current costs and practice.
  In this context, too, watch for any indications of time scales in a mini-case. For example, if the case indicates or specifies a plan of action to cover the next twelve months, make sure that your plan covers *precisely* this period, not the next three months or the next five years. Where a series of actions is required over the requisite period, your answer should demonstrate clearly the timing and sequence of these actions over the specified time period.
- *Clearly state any assumptions you have made.*
  Often in case studies, you will need to make assumptions, and in this respect the mini-cases are no different. The examiners will be happy to accept any assumption *so long as it is reasonable in the context of the case.* You should clearly specify *any* assumptions you have made in arriving at your proposals for courses of action. In fact, so long as your assumptions meet the 'reasonable' criterion, you can use your assumptions to your advantage. An example will serve to illustrate:

The following communications plan for the company is based on the following assumptions:

- The annual rate of overall market growth will continue at 3 per cent per annum for the next three years.
- All new products are produced to BS 5270.
- Potential new competitors will find it difficult to enter the market quickly.

Used wisely and creatively, assumptions can help you to clear away any considerations which, though important, are peripheral to the particular aspects on which the questions centre. They can also be used to support the line of argument in your answers.

- *Suggest specific courses of action.*
  Again, in line with what the mini-cases are intended to test, your answers should indicate *solutions to problems* through clearly specified courses of action rather than simply the identification of the problems themselves.
  In most questions, the action required will be explicit in the questions themselves. For example:

  'Write a brief for an export market research plan with the aim of identifying overseas target markets . . .'

  In some questions, alternative courses of action may be open to the company in the case: indeed, you may be asked to identify these. However, wherever possible and appropriate, you should be careful not to use a mere listing of alternatives as a means of avoiding a commitment to a particular alternative. At the very least you should prioritize your alternatives and give supporting reasons for your choice.
- *Do not over-complicate your answers.*
  Essentially the mini-cases are not over-complicated. They are testing your ability to *apply* key concepts and techniques from each of the subject areas. Keep your answers brief, to the point and in the format specified. Above all, do not over-complicate your answers.

To summarize some of the most important considerations in actually tackling a mini-case, here are the key points to remember when preparing your answers:

- Avoid 'waffle' and extended general introductions.
- Note constraints and time scales.
- State assumptions.
- Propose relevant action.
- Do not over-complicate.
- Answer the actual question set.

We can now start to see how these considerations work in practice. Before moving on to examine worked examples of mini-cases in the next chapter, we have included a further two sample mini-cases, this time from the Diploma level Planning and Control and International Marketing Strategy papers. To help illustrate the main points of the suggested format for tackling the mini-cases, we have analysed the comments of the external examiner in some detail and have annotated the key learning points.

3.3 Two further sample mini-cases

The Chartered Institute of Marketing

Diploma In Marketing

Strategic Marketing Management Planning and Control

Time: 09.30–12.30

Date: Monday 12th December 1994

3 Hours Duration

(Note the overall time allocation)

SYLLABUS 94

(You can't avoid the mini-case)

This examination is in two sections.

Part A is compulsory, based on a mini-case and worth 50% of total marks.

(50% of the marks means 50% of the examination time)

Part B has eight questions, select three. Each answer will be given equal marks totalling 50% of the whole for the paper.

(No marks for repeating questions)

DO NOT repeat the question in your answer but show clearly the number of the question attempted on appropriate pages of the answer book.

(Leave your analysis out of the answer)

Rough workings should be included in the answer book and ruled through after use.

The copyright of all The Chartered Institute of Marketing examination material is held by the Institute. No Case Study or Questions may be reproduced without its prior permission which must be obtained in writing.

DIPLOMA IN MARKETING
STRATEGIC MARKET MANAGEMENT: PLANNING AND CONTROL

Part A

Olworth Leisure Centre

There are several hundred leisure/sports/recreation centres in the UK jointly provided by public authorities and local education authorities.

A typical centre includes a sports hall, a swimming pool, two gymnasia, squash courts, sauna, solarium, lounge bar, games area and is located in a surrounding fielded area for track sports and athletics. The indoor sports hall would be marked out for badminton, netball, volley ball, etc. and might be large enough for an occasional indoor tennis court.

Olworth is a population centre of about 10 000 inhabitants and considered to be an area of high deprivation and isolation, resulting in relatively high rates of crime and vandalism. Most of the menfolk work in nearby factories, often on a shift basis.

The district council responsible for Olworth is considering building a leisure centre in the conurbation for use by its local population, but with the hope of attracting people from surrounding villages and hamlets within a radius of ten miles with an additional population of 12 000. Due to financial and other constraints building is likely to take place in three phases over a total of three years.

Obviously objectives for the provision and use of leisure centre services are not necessarily based upon profit as such, although a level of income contributing considerably towards running costs is projected.

Leisure centre services are not always in a situation of economic balance where demand matches supply, and it is not unusual for some activities/ facilities to be overbooked, e.g. squash and swimming, while other minority sports facilities are grossly under-utilized. A major problem facing local authority-provided centres has been the maximization of usage during weekdays. In the evenings and weekends, with the demand from the general public and various clubs and organizations, the space more than sells itself.

Olworth Council see this project somewhat as a marketing planning and control exercise. They are anxious to achieve a good match between supply and demand and are aware of the importance of the four Ps (place being in the sense of timing of a given leisure facility and its duration as well as location) in this aim. They have asked a local college to put this project to their Marketing course members in the hope of obtaining some practical help in the form of a marketing plan. As a <u>member of this course</u> your individual task is to:

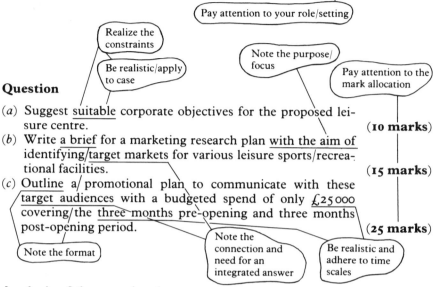

Question

(a) Suggest <u>suitable</u> corporate objectives for the proposed leisure centre. **(10 marks)**

(b) Write <u>a brief</u> for a marketing research plan <u>with the aim of</u> <u>identifying/target</u> markets for various leisure sports/recreational facilities. **(15 marks)**

(c) <u>Outline</u> a/ promotional plan to communicate with these target audiences with a budgeted spend of only £25 000 covering/the <u>three months</u> pre-opening and three months post-opening period. **(25 marks)**

Analysis of the examiner's report

Again, many of the points which have been highlighted seem rather obvious. With this in mind, however, now let us have a look at the examiner's report.

Planning and control – examiner's report

Olworth Leisure Centre

General comments

Overall, more candidates are demonstrating adequacy in the professionalism of their answers and general approach. Very few candidates unnecessarily <u>repeated</u> <u>questions</u> before answering. Failures tend to <u>show</u> marked weaknesses in <u>one section of the paper</u> rather than both. A good proportion of examinees demonstrating an adequate knowledge of the syllabus in Section II were found <u>wanting</u> in their ability to <u>apply/this</u> knowledge to the\practical case situation. Often students who were clearly lacking in sufficient knowledge to gain passes in Section II did somewhat better in the practical case situation.

Failures also showed a tendency to 'waffle'; that is, to avoid directly addressing the question, spending at least the <u>first page</u> of their answers on general introductions. Many students did <u>SWOT</u> or situational analyses or <u>introductions</u> to Section I. Candidates are urged to recognize that examiners are looking for points relevant to the question in order to award marks and that scene-setting gains them few, if any, marks and is essentially wasting valuable time. Equally students, in making a valid point, should avoid subsequent over-elaboration of that single point over the next page or more before making the next valid point. This often leads to answers four pages or more long, containing only four valid points-out of the 10 the examiner is looking for. Such an approach, apart from failing to gain sufficient marks to pass quantitatively, also demonstrates a failure to plan answers, which is depressing in a subject testing planning and control.

Make what you write score marks

Substance scores points

Plan your work and work your plan

A disappointing number of examinees failed to adopt report format in answering Section I. Essay format was completely inappropriate for stating corporate objectives, for presenting a marketing brief and even more so for an outline promotional plan. Incredibly, some candidates used essay form for the checklist called for in Section II, Question 1.

Wrong format

Adopt report style

Some failure to understand what is meant by terms such as a brief, marketing mix, promotion mix, test marketing, corporate, etc. was apparent. When given a choice, candidates should avoid answering questions using terms they do not properly understand as such basic mistakes tend to deflate the mark the examiners can properly award.

It is hoped that future examinees reading this report will also read other examiners' reports which contain valuable points on what to avoid in their endeavours to pass the examination in this subject and that they will also avail themselves of the opportunity to acquire specimen answers to previous papers so as to make themselves aware of the content and standard of answers ideally required as well as of the approach looked for in answering particular types of questions.

A tip for exam preparation

Part A (mini-case)

Know your subject

In answering question (a) many candidates showed themselves unable to distinguish between objectives, strategies and tactics. Others adopted a functional rather than corporate approach. Some candidates gave just one objective (ignoring the question's request for objectives) and some gave a long list of trivialities, the record being 23!

Ignoring the question

The main cause of failure for question (b) was a lack of understanding of how to write a brief in the first place and, secondly, ignorance of the content of marketing research plans. Many candidates failed to consider that valuable information could be obtained in the form of secondary data, especially by looking at the nature and success of other leisure centres in similar areas. A depressing number of candidates suggested acquiring primary data on just about everything but crucial facts such as how many respondents would visit the centre, to use which particular facilities, at what frequencies, based on what price expectations and what media would reach them effectively. Briefs should, of course, allude to timing and cost considerations.

(Relevance)

(Remember time scales)

(Consider scale of operation and cost constraints)

Answers to question (c) were, on the whole, well done, with most candidates sketching in costed media schedules split into pre- and post-opening activities. There were also some good creative ideas, particularly from overseas candidates, who suggested PA vehicles touring streets, audio-visual presentations to clubs, etc. While the approaching of regional TV for free publicity on the grounds of news value was acceptable, the idea that this would provide continuous coverage was untenable. Unfortunately, too many candidates from overseas suggested paid-for TV advertising at ridiculously low costs, failing to realize that the budget would not permit such an expensive promotional activity and that *regional* TV would not in any case be cost-effective for a *local* sports centre, neither would *national* sports/leisure magazine advertising. Too many candidates also omitted any check on promotional expenditure effectiveness in their outline plans.

(Failure to note constraints)

(Lack of realism)

(Lack of professionalism)

You will no doubt note from the examiners' comments that failure to spot and/or take account of the seemingly 'obvious' points underpin many of the criticisms. You can also see the importance of adopting a practical/professional rather than academic approach. For example, note the frequent comments as to budgeting, costing and timing, all of which would be important if you were actually in a business situation.

To summarize, you should now be beginning to appreciate the format of mini-cases; what is expected of you in the examination; the key skills required; the overall approach to tackling mini-cases; and the pitfalls to avoid.

In order to reinforce and add to some of the key learning points from our analysis of the Olworth Leisure Centre case and examiner's report, there now follows our final sample mini-case. This time we have selected a Diploma level International Marketing Strategy paper and have concentrated on the examiner's report.

DIPLOMA IN MARKETING
INTERNATIONAL MARKETING STRATEGY

Part A

The MacHamish Distillery

As he looked down the winding road in the remote Highland glen where his family had been distilling whisky for several generations, Angus MacHamish sampled the latest batch. 'Well up to standard,' he said. 'In five years it will be reasonable, and then in ten we can bottle and market it. I wonder if we ought to increase the quantity in the next few batches?' His father, recently retired from the business, was more inclined to be cautious. 'All the big distilleries have had their fingers burned with the fall in sales since 1979 – nearly 20 per cent down since then. Everyone overproduced and is overstocked by two years' requirements, and production is cut to half what it was.' 'But that is for the standard, blended grain whiskies – premium brands like ours have maintained their sales and even increased them over that time,' said Angus.

Whisky is produced from cereals, which are fermented and then distilled. The cereals used vary with the type of whisky required. Bourbon and rye, produced in the USA, must contain at least 15 per cent of maize and 51 per cent of rye respectively in their cereal content, while the true Scotch whisky is produced from two main bases – malt, which is made from malted barley only, with no additional cereals, and is twice distilled by a batch process; and grain whisky, which is distilled in a continuous process from a mixture of malted and unmalted barley and other grains, usually maize. Arising from this, and apart from a very small quantity of pure grain whisky, three types of Scotch are normally produced for consumption:

1. A single malt whisky – from one distillery only.
2. A blended malt whisky – malts from several distilleries.
3. Blended Scotch whiskies – blends of malt and grain whiskies.

The malts accounted for only 2 per cent of the sales volume; the other 98 per cent of the 251 million litres produced in 1993 being blended.

These are further subdivided into:

(a) De luxe premium brands (75% proof)	–3%
(b) Standard brands (70% proof)	–80%
(c) Own label and cheap brands (65% proof)	–15%

The production and blending of different whiskies to give desirable and consistent products is an art learned only by experience, for whiskies made even by the same method and from the same raw materials in two different distilleries will be unlikely to taste the same. So far it has proved difficult to equal the quality of Scotch whisky anywhere else in the world, although Japan has been striving hard.

The decline in the blended Scotch whisky sales can be ascribed to several causes common over much of the world – the economic recession and heavy duties payable were significant, but even more the ageing profile of whisky drinkers. Over one-third of buyers were in the 45 to 64 age group, and the younger drinkers preferred gins and vodkas, or lighter drinks, to whiskies.

Exports too had declined in volume by 9 per cent between 1987 and 1993; the European Union member countries were the largest market in terms of value, taking some £230m out of a total export value of £864m; and the USA was the largest market (30 per cent) by volume. This was followed by Japan, in second place by volume of sales; and to lesser degrees by France, West Germany, Spain and Canada.

As might be expected with such individualistic products and fragmented markets, branding was very important. The total of advertising expenditure by whisky firms was some £20m in 1994 – the seven largest distilleries spent some £8m. Below-the-line promotions, such as the sponsorship of sports events, were also widely used. One-third of all UK sales were made through public houses and hotels; of the remaining two-thirds over half of all sales were now made through grocers and supermarkets, and over a third through off-licences and wine merchants; while other outlets included a significant proportion, usually of the premium brands, through duty-free shops at ports. The MacHamish distillery spent some £100000 on limited press advertising, as all its sales were through high-class wine merchants in the UK only.

Unlike his father, Angus wished to build on the established strength of MacHamish, and, in view of the static situation in the UK, wanted to consider overseas markets. While some stock could be immediately available, any significant increase in sales would be a long-term operation, allowing plenty of time to develop the operation. He would now require advice.

The questions below draw attention to some international aspects of the situation, *all* of which you are required to answer. There are other aspects relevant to the possible development of the firm's activities which you may wish to consider, and credit will be given for suitable observations.

Question

Advise MacHamish on:

(a) A suitable procedure to find possible markets overseas for their whisky. **(20 marks)**

(b) An outline plan for selecting appropriate distribution channels. **(20 marks)**

(c) Promotional activities. **(10 marks)**

Analysis of the examiner's report

International Marketing Strategy – examiner's report

General comments

As in most examinations, particular questions are set and worded in such a way as to not only test the student's knowledge of the relevant area and his or her ability to apply that knowledge in given circumstances, but also to be able to do so in managerial, decision-making fashion. To this end, the questions in both Parts A and B are so phrased as to require some definite approach or framework in the answer.

Note the examiner's objectives

Clear thinking, clear logic are needed

Report format is essential

Considerable latitude is given in the actual contents as long as they are appropriate, but at the end of the question or Part the examiner has to ask him or herself whether or not the student has actually answered the question as set. All too frequently a particular word or phrase is noted, but then the actual question is mentally rephrased or rewritten by the student, who thereby misses the actual points required. However correct the contents of such work may be, few marks can be given if the actual question is not answered.

Note, there are no 'right' answers in case work

The key reason for failure

An alternative, but equally fatal approach, is for the student to seize upon a particular word or phrase and then to write anything and everything about it, irrespective of the relevance or application. In this area, an improvement has been noted, however, that there are fewer examples of complete checklists being regurgitated without consideration of the relevance of individual items, and this does indicate an improvement in the application of the managerial approach.

Note the examiner's objectives

Part A (mini-case)

The MacHamish Distillery

The need to read and understand the questions carefully before answering is particularly relevant to at least the first two questions in the mini-case. Surely it should not be necessary to state what is meant by a 'procedure' and a 'plan'? But the number of students who completely ignored any sequence or direction in the methods to be used, let alone the steps or actions which would be dependent on a previous activity, cost many their pass marks. Similarly, a plan of any kind is an outline of actions proposed, again sequential, which would lead from some defined objective to some control to ensure a successful operation. In too

Read these before you start reading the mini-case to help to focus your thoughts

Have a planning structure prepared that you can use if requested

Consider the cost implications of your recommendations. Remember to balance the scale of your suggestions with the financial constraints of the organization

Identify the constraints which limit the company's market potential

many cases these approaches were just not followed. Where a 'procedure' was outlined, all too often the result was a full market research across the whole world, eliminating some countries for one reason, then a second batch for another, until by dint of much hard work, time and certainly far more money than Mac-Hamish would ever have been able to spend, the one or two countries for the first attack were produced. This type of answer is not wrong – it is usually too general-ized to be so – but it is not all that realistic for a firm of MacHamish's indicated size and resources, let alone the unique product itself and the limited and special-ized potential market for it.

Realism must prevail

Virtually no useful references were made to two particularly limiting parameters: that of the ten-year production period and the actual quantities available either for immediate sale or at particular periods in the future. No actual figures were given – or necessary – but a reference to the consideration of the stock figures and future availability over the next ten years would have been the basis for the answers to all three parts of the question, to give some element of realism to the actual distribution channels or the promotions selected.

The misreading of the question continued to be a major cause of low marks in part (*b*). A plan was required to enable a selection to be made of the most appropriate distribution channel(s). There could have been several quite reasonable distribution methods pos-sible and acceptable; but what was *not* required was a complete list of all possible export methods (including local production overseas, either directly or under licence!) without any attempt to discriminate and choose between them; and presented as a list without any indication of a selection procedure. How to organ-ize the selection procedure was the requirement here, not just the range of choices possible.

Another classic error

For part (*c*) 'promotional activities' were left wide open for any appropriate treatment. Unfortunately, far too many students were content with repeating broadly the methods already mentioned in the study without any evaluation or development. Few attempted, for instance, to quantify, however crudely, the funds avail-able or needed for the overseas operation, let alone to consider what the actual tasks and objectives of the promotion were to be. In this, too, a consideration of the particular channel characteristics would have been appropriate.

Justify your approach. Show the rationale for your recommendations

Be clear on the purpose and the means of achieving it

As a final observation, all three parts should relate to each other to form a coherent whole; the promotional activities should have been evaluated and appropriate for use as part of the distribution selection process, and this again should have been related to the market selection cases.

As a postscript, the senior examiner is still trying to work out what would be involved in the case of one answer received, which recommended that MacHamish should emphasize the provision of 'a full after-sales service, including the provision of spare parts'! Presumably for legless drinkers?

$$\star \quad \star \quad \star \quad \star \quad \star$$

3.4 Summary

You should by now have a good feel for what the mini-cases are all about, how to approach them and what the examiners are looking for.

We are now ready to move on to the next step in preparing you for the mini-case examinations, namely the introduction of worked examples of mini-cases.

4 Answering the mini-case: worked examples of mini-cases

In this chapter we present a number of worked examples of sample mini-cases. Each of these sample cases is taken from an actual CIM examination. The idea of these worked examples is for you to observe for yourself the application of the approach and techniques which we have discussed by a hypothetical 'well prepared' candidate.

In order to achieve this we have traced through what might be the thought processes of our hypothetical candidate, together with guidance as to the sort of analysis and note making which the candidate would need to go through in preparing an answer. These are then developed into a full specimen answer, followed, finally, by a set of printed notes on the main learning points from the worked example.

You should note that the notes which accompany each of the sample cases are for your guidance only and would, of course, not normally be included in analysing and answering an actual examination case.

We have started with a mini-case from the Diploma level International Marketing Management Strategy paper, working through it in some considerable detail. This is followed by a second sample case, this time using a Sales Operations case from the Advanced Certificate level. Here we summarize the approach that our candidate might have taken in preparing his or her answers.

Our third case is taken from the Marketing Operations syllabus. By the time you reach this third case you should be reasonably confident about how to approach the mini-cases. Therefore, for this final specimen case we have simply pointed to the key points to consider in arriving at a set of solutions to the problems posed in the case.

You should read through each of these worked examples of cases at least twice in order to reap maximum value from them. Later on, when you come to tackle mini-cases on your own, you can return to the worked examples in this chapter to remind yourself of the suggested approach.

DIPLOMA IN MARKETING
INTERNATIONAL MARKETING STRATEGY

Part A

Karlstein GmbH

Karlstein GmbH was formed some twenty years ago by a metal-processing manufacturer based in Hanover, West Germany.

The company manufactures bathroom fixtures and fittings, principally for plumbing application (including taps, joints and shower fittings).

A wide range of end users exists, including domestic householders and industrial/institutional buyers.

In the last year the company achieved market shares of 36 per cent in West Germany, 10 per cent in France and 3 per cent in Belgium. In addition, 5 per cent of total production was shipped to a major wholesaler in Miami, USA. Total turnover exceeds 80 million DM.

The wide range of fittings varies in size, style, colour, metal and plastic finishings to occupy bottom and top end market positions.

A feasibility study has recently been completed to assess the potential of the UK market. Encouraging results have now stimulated the company to, pursue actively the UK market with a target date for entry in ten months' time.

Question

(*a*) Advise the company of the options open to achieve UK market entry.
(*b*) Outline the potential 'difficulties' involved with each option.
(*c*) Select and justify a method of market entry and give a detailed account of the physical distribution implications.

★ ★ ★ ★ ★

Guidance notes on sample mini-case 1

1 Familiarization with case and questions

Note: The case chosen here for analysis is deliberately short as this is a feature of mini-cases.

1.1 Before you write anything, you should first read through the case and questions *at least twice*. A good tip is to read the questions asked before you read the case. By so doing, you will read the case with some idea of the issues that you will have to address.

1.2 Having acquainted yourself with the content of the case and the ques-

tions, read through the case slowly, underlining or highlighting the key issues and salient facts. At this stage, you should confine yourself to general but succinct observations, not extended general observations.
Here are some examples from the case:

- Twenty-year-old West German manufacturer.
- Products manufactured: bathroom fixtures and fittings in metal and plastic finishes.
- Markets served: domestic householders; industrial and institutional buyers.
- Wide range of fittings in different sizes, styles and colours to suit as wide a proportion of the market as possible.
- Market shares:

$$\%$$

West Germany = 36
France = 10
Belgium = 3
USA (Miami) = 5

- Total turnover = 80 million DM plus.
- Turnover to markets stated must be in the order of 25 million or so DM.
  - Decision has been taken to enter the UK market with target entry date in ten months' time

Note: You do not need to write down these facts and observations as this would waste examination time. It is sufficient that you merely underline them where appropriate or use a highlighting pen.

2 *Analysis of questions/instructions*

You should now read through the instructions and questions again very carefully. In this sample case you should have noted the following:

2.1 The number of questions together with the mark, and therefore time allocation for each (here, three questions with marks not ascribed, so it is fair to assume that each will be marked $33\frac{1}{3}\%$). This means that the time to be allocated is half an hour on each question, minus the time spent reading through and understanding the case. Remember, at the Diploma level the mini-case accounts for 50 of the 100 marks available. So on this case each part of the question is worth just over 16 marks.
This time we shall comment more briefly on the overall approach.

In many mini-cases unequal marks are awarded to individual questions, and in such cases it is advisable to allocate time in accordance with the ratio of marks to be given to each individual question.
As a guide, you should allocate your time like this:

Time allowed for mini-case = 90 minutes
Less preparation/reading time = 15 minutes
Time available for writing answers = 75 minutes

2.2 All questions are specific and need to have a structured answer in the

form of observations and/or recommendations:
- Methods of UK market entry.
- Difficulties involved with each option.
- Select and justify one method from those cited and detail physical distribution implications.

2.3 You are not given a specific role to play in the company other than that of adviser/consultant.

2.4 Any information/instructions as to timing, budgets, constraints, etc. in the questioning should be noted and adhered to. In this case such information is not added, but sometimes a constraint like a 'limited budget' is referred to.

2.5 Any information or instructions as to format should be noted. No specific reference is made to this in this particular case, so you should adopt report-style format. Report format is the usual style to adopt, so ensure that you are fully versed in your 'favourite' report style before the examination. We discuss the preparation of reports later.

3 Analysis of case material in relation to the questions

It was mentioned earlier that now, and only now, is the candidate in a position to work through the case material in detail. You should now be fully familiar with the case, the questions and your role. You can now proceed to analyse the case in the context of the questions asked.

Mini-cases, as the title implies, contain only limited information, and consequently the amount of analysis that you can undertake is limited. In the context of the specimen case and questions under review, here are some of the key elements that you should consider:

3.1 You have the total sales turnover (80 million plus DM). You have the market shares for certain countries.

3.2 The immediate problem is how to attain market entry into the UK successfully. This will be at a cost in terms of logistics, promotion, etc.

3.3 The company has experience of marketing in non-West German markets.

3.4 Recommendations as to developing the UK market will need to reflect assumptions as to the problems associated with each method of distribution within the context of the products to be marketed.

Note on the analysis

This is the kind of analysis and thought processes that our candidate should have gone through in preparing to answer the questions on the Karlstein mini-case. You should also note that in illustrating the analysis we have necessarily made more detailed and expansive notes than would be possible or necessary in the examination itself.

In the examination paper you would simply be preparing rough notes and pointers in your analysis (normally at the head of the paper in rough pencil notes – deleted after you have completed the answer). Remember that the examiner is interested only in your answers to the specific questions and not in the rough notes on your analysis. Doing it in this manner is useful, because quite often when you are writing the answer further thoughts might occur to you. Such thoughts can then be added to the rough notes to be included in the appropriate part of your narrative. Quite often, too, thoughts occur to you afterwards. Although it might not look aesthetically pleasing, the best course to adopt here is to ensure that you leave sufficient space between points so that it is possible to insert the forgotten point afterwards without 'crowding' the appearance of your paper too much. Otherwise, leave sufficient space between individual parts of your answer and put an asterisk at the place where you wish to insert the extra information (with an appropriate note to the examiner, e.g. 'Please see additional point at the end of this section for insertion here').

4 Preparation of answers

The following is a suggested solution of the Karlstein mini-case illustrating the way in which our candidate might have set about answering the specific questions. First, simply read through the answer shown, remembering of course, that this represents only a sample of a variety of possible ways of resolving the issues in the questions.

International marketing strategy

Answer

A. General observations

1 The company has a significant market position in Europe; an apparent market strength to operate on.
2 It has substantial international experience.
3 The product has a wide range of applications; the company is not a specialist. The product is a general type.
4 Therefore, it is a multiproduct company. Also, it has brand recognition through establishment within the market.
5 The management is shrewd and forward-thinking because of the feasibility study.
6 The *stimulus* that is driving the situation is that the company is expanding and that there is planned growth.
7 A planned international organization is taking place with determination to penetrate the UK market.

B. Options

(*a*) Direct export.
(*b*) To set up a manufacturing base in the UK.
(*c*) The appointment of sales distribution.
(*d*) Joint venture with existing UK company with established distribution channel.
(*e*) To manufacture under licence.

(*f*) To set up own sales industry.

(*g*) To set up a pioneering sales force to test market the product.

(*h*) *Acquisition   forward integration*: (distributor and wholesaler with existing sales force)

   horizontal integration: (a UK-based manufacturer perhaps 51 per cent only to buy the controlling interest) – it may be less than 50 per cent – we only need the percentage that can control.

International problems:

The time it takes to:

• get recognized
• obtain distribution
• obtain market position.

Acquisition or mergers are only good for well-established companies. They are not good for young blood.

Difficulties of each option:

(*a*) *direct exporting*

   • market acceptance
   • market resistance to a foreign brand name
   • time to get distribution penetration
   • control (little control on growth)
   • little trade penetration into the product and end-user application
   • delays in payment

(*b*) *New manufacturing base*

   • investment
   • location
   • training of workforce
   • employment of qualified staff
   • obtaining the correct advice (on location of base and benefits of different choices)
   • time delay to obtain market acceptance, trade acceptance
   • overall risks of new venture

(*c*) *Sales distribution of agents*

   • difficult to get good agents (biggest may not be best)
   • the on-cost of appointing the agents has to be passed on to the final price to the consumer
   • the agent may find difficulty in getting the product accepted (further market resistance)
   • the performance of overtime may vary
   • communication can be fragmented
   • maintenance of sales effort
   • problem of motivation

- the loyalty to the company is based purely on financial return
- agents may sell competing products

(*d*) *Joint venture*

- difficult to establish mutual commitment and understanding
- finding the right partner
- problems that arise after the joint venture is sealed, e.g. politics, power fight
- the need to achieve common objectives through a common interest
- the need to establish bases for profit repatriation and result contribution

(*e*) *Licensing*

- the appropriateness with reference to the market
- maintenance and achievement of standards
- the need to determine the real cost-effectiveness
- loss of control
- the reputation of the product is at stake
- marketing is in the hands of a third party
- it is inappropriate for a multiproduct company with highly technical specification required
- it may conflict with the object of the licensor
- tax disadvantages with reference to royalties that must be paid
- the requirement of self-franchise over the licence and the link limits to growth potential

(*f*) *Sales subsidiary abroad* (quite a sensible option)

- investment
- time lag (in getting to understand the market, building the sales system and sales base)
- correct staffing
- need for pioneering
- the level of financial risk and meeting the objectives specified by the German company

(*g*) *Pioneering sales force or export sales force*

- need to integrate in a foreign country
- cultural differences
- gaining personal level acceptance
- to overcome the adjustment of the product to meet market requirements
- setting up a sales system
- maintaining motivation

(*h*) *Acquisition* (difficulties are short-term)

- acquiring the right company
- securing investment rather than incurring additional cost
- getting the right acquisition profile

Suggested method of market entry is by acquisition and the reasons behind it are:

(*a*) Effective use of time in securing market penetration.
(*b*) Existing market position.
(*c*) Existing market contact.
(*d*) Existing sales system.
(*e*) Existing distribution channels.
(*f*) Knowledge of marketing institutions and facilities.
(*g*) Existing customer groupings.
(*h*) A ready-made company where the purchaser is buying years of invest-ment in terms of corporate development.
(*i*) In short, it is a cost-effective method in gaining market entry and securing an established market position.

Physical distribution implications of the selected option

1 The need to standardize the paperwork system between the companies.
2 The need to set up an inventory system between the exporting and importing countries.
3 To ensure economical order quantities and delivery.
4 To use the most cost-effective method of distribution and yet maintain customer service levels.
5 To set a level for distribution form to meet the defined distribution objectives.
6 Road transportation (containerization using roll-on roll-off facilities for bulk orders) and rail transportation for smallest specialist orders.

The overall implication of the total distribution system is one of cost control.

Because the option has been selected the acquired company's distribution network will be fully utilized until such time as an alternative is required.

This then is a very detailed analysis of our first worked case. We can now move on to a second analysis, this time based on an Advanced Certificate Level – Sales Operations case.

Notes on the answer

1 See how we have adopted the appropriate type of format for the answer.
2 It is made quite clear from the use of headings which questions are being addressed.
3 Any assumptions are clearly stated.
4 In order to put the case in the setting a 'general observations' section is included at the beginning. This does not necessarily score marks, but it does allow a smoother transition into the case analysis and it demonstrates that you, the candidate, have clear thought processes. More to the point, it might save time later in the analysis as you will not have to go into long explanations of why you are making such recommendations.

5 Where necessary and appropriate, any detailed parts of the initial analysis can be included as a separate appendix (not necessary in this case).
6 Clear courses of action have been suggested within the constraints of the case scenario.

Undoubtedly, this answer would have scored high marks in an examination. Mini-cases, however, often demand variations of this basic style. To illustrate this point we shall now examine in turn two further mini-case examples.

Allwarm (Knitting) Limited

Allwarm (Knitting) Limited has been producing and selling knitting yarns for some eighty years. Throughout this period the company has always sold its products through specialist shops and through some departmental stores under the brand name 'Allwarm'. The product range is very extensive and includes a wide range of colours and yarn types. All the company's hand-knitting yarns are produced using pure new wool or blends of wool and more 'exclusive' fibres such as mohair and angora. The company has always taken great pride in the quality of its products and believes that its brand name is well known and well respected by customers and the trade alike.

After a lull in the early 1980s when hand knitting became less popular, recent years have witnessed a return to knitting at home. One reason for this has been that it has become 'fashionable' to wear hand-knitted garments. Younger women in particular like the idea of being able to knit an individual garment using top-quality material at a fraction of the cost of a similar shop-bought item. Major fashion houses have recently made knitwear a prominent feature of their collections.

These changes in fashion are reflected in the consumption statistics for hand-knitting yarns:

United Kingdom hand-knitting yarn consumption
(including natural and artificial fibres and mixed fibres)

Year	Sales (million kg)
1983	10.0
1984	9.8
1985	9.6
1986	11.6
1987	12.9
1988	14.0
1989	15.1
1990	15.3
1991	15.2
1992	15.6
1993	15.6
1994	15.1
1995	15.3

Despite this growth, Allwarm's market share of the total market has diminished over the past five years. In 1991 their market share was 6 per cent of the total volume, but by 1995 this had fallen to 4 per cent.

The company commissioned a market research study which found that although total hand-knitting yarn consumption was steady between 1991 and 1995, of the total amount sold yarns incorporating artificial fibres were increasing at the expense of natural fibre yarns. The principal reason for this was found to be the price advantage of artificial yarns over natural yarns (approximately 30 per cent cheaper). The study also found that there had been a shift by distributors (especially department stores) from stocking branded yarns to unbranded yarns as they were generally cheaper. It was also discovered that many of the cheaper hand-knitting yarns are being sold through market outlets – many as manufacturers' 'seconds' (i.e. yarns which would not pass the stringent quality tests carried out by Allwarm).

Allwarm does not own any distribution outlets and a UK sales force of ten sells direct to specialist knitting-yarn shops, accounting for 90 per cent of sales, and department stores, which account for the remainder. The concentration is historical because Allwarm feels that the specialist shop is the most appropriate way to sell their high-quality branded yarns. Many customers often seek advice from retailers when they purchase hand-knitting yarns. Allwarm believes that its reputation in the trade is such that specialist retailers are likely to recommend its products to such customers in preference to cheaper unbranded or mixed yarn products.

Question

(a) Advise Allwarm (Knitting) Limited what to do over a one-year period to counteract falling sales. **(25 marks)**
(b) Advise Allwarm (Knitting) Limited how to restructure its marketing process in general, and its selling and distribution arrangements in particular, in order to take account of changes that are taking place in the marketplace. **(25 marks)**

★ ★ ★ ★ ★

Approach

As in virtually all mini-cases, the approach required is dictated by the circumstances of the particular case and the questions asked on it. Our candidate on the Allwarm Knitting case, therefore, should read the signposts provided by the examiner.

The questions are actually in a logical sequence. First of all, efforts need to be made to stop sales falling further. This will need to be accompanied by a restructuring of marketing in general in the company and selling and distribution arrangements in particular.

A sensible approach for our candidate would have been to first assess all the information in the case which is relevant to the issues raised by the questions. For example, it is clear that the following are among some of the key reasons for loss of market share in particular:

- Uncompetitive prices
- Changes in distribution

- A possible lack of awareness of changes/trends in the marketplace on the part of Allwarm's management until, of course, the market research was commissioned.

Clearly steps will need to be taken to redress the following levels of sales and market share, but again there is evidence in the case of some of the problems that will have to be addressed by Allwarm and hence in our candidate's recommendations. In particular:

- Clearly the competition (especially on price) is fierce.
- They may be out of touch with how (and where) customers purchase.
- The organization of the sales force appears to be very traditional.
- In line with the above, new channels of distribution and selling skills may be required.

Answer

Allwarm (Knitting) Limited

(a) *Counteracting falling sales*

1 *Introduction*
   This report considers the action required by Allwarm to counteract falling sales of their products, despite a steady market. Clearly, Allwarm seems to have let events overtake the company without doing anything about it, and in being so sales-oriented and not marketing-oriented they have failed to notice the danger signals that a good marketing-led company would have identified. The problem therefore lies with the attitude of the company, which has almost been complacent in ignoring the changing trends of the market.

2 *Short-term solutions*
   2.1 There does not appear to be a clear marketing strategic plan – it is essential that Allwarm produces a clear integrated plan of how market share can be built and the market's potential realized. A starting point would be to consider fully the market research recently carried out and to analyse the secondary data which exist within customer records and accounts. This will indicate in which market segments the company can make a swift impact.

   2.2 Many tactics are possible to increase sales levels in the short term. The use of sales promotions is very effective in the short term, and these can be used in several ways.

      2.2.1 *Trade.* Allwarm must encourage trade outlets to increase stocks of its product. This may mean some research being carried out by Allwarm to determine and take a closer look at how organizational buyers purchase. It may also be beneficial to ensure that trade outlets merchandise the yarn more effectively and push it harder to potential customers.

      2.2.2 *Consumer.* These promotions can take the form of incentives to purchase (for example, the use of price packs, i.e. three for the price of two; coupons; money-back offers if you spend over a certain amount).

2.3 In addition, sales management should consider the attitude of the sales force, and the immediate impact they could have on short-term sales levels.

 2.3.1 *The effective use of sales targets and quotas.* Sales managers must set quantitative objectives expressed in terms of sales values or units of product in order to monitor the performance against desired standards. The short-term effectiveness of such tactics can be enhanced by attractive incentives to outperform these specified standards.

 2.3.2 *The use of effective advertising campaigns* can support the short-term initiative to increase sales. Use of local radio or regional press in conjunction with a special sales promotion can enhance short-term sales.

 2.3.3 *The use of direct mail properly targeted to potential customers.*

 2.3.4 *In-store demonstrations and exhibitions* can be used effectively to create awareness and interest in the product.

3 *Conclusions*

The company would be well advised to establish a more balanced marketing mix and a much stronger marketing orientation. While short-term measures may 'kick start' the product sales, there is a clear need for a longer-term strategy to be devised. In devising such a strategy, comprehensive market research ought to be carried out to determine:

3.1 Who is buying the product (geographically, demographically) and usage rates.

3.2 Perceived benefits of the yarn,

3.3 Effectiveness of the sales force,

3.4 Competitor analysis.

Short-term activity needs to move towards below-the-line activities such as in-store campaigns, leaflets, trade advertising and sales force incentives to increase the market share of Allwarm.

Suggestions on restructuring marketing, selling and distribution arrangements

Introduction

Clearly, Allwarm should change its orientation to that of marketing orientation, which means looking at changes in the marketplace. It would pay Allwarm to involve all company employees in its new strategies, and if this means the establishment of a new marketing department then this should be done. The following should be considered:

1 A full appraisal of the marketplace should be carried out. The use of market research, product research, promotional and distribution research via primary (newly commissioned) or secondary data is appropriate. Without such research, the company will be unable to make important strategic decisions.

1.1 Are the company's products still in favour/fashion?
1.2 Are purchasing patterns and trends within the marketplace changing?
1.3 Is there a defined market segment for the product?

Once answers have been determined, strategic decisions can be made on whether to introduce new products – perhaps an artificial fibre yarn to the product mix to enhance the product portfolio. In addition, the introduction of a new product range may enable the company to increase its selling outlets.

2 Once research has been carried out and a strategic plan formulated, the company would be well advised to inform all company employees via in-house bulletins, group meetings and quality circles.
3 Distribution research also needs to consider changing patterns of distribution and how new channels need to be considered.
   3.1 Allwarm's current policy of selective distribution needs to be examined. Such a policy limits Allwarm, and the marketplace can be developed further via outlets other than specialist shops and department stores. Allwarm could consider forms of integration by perhaps purchasing shops and selling the yarn direct. In addition, Allwarm could consider links with garment producers, in particular fashion products.
   3.2 Allwarm should consider the mix of distribution with its direct selling operation. It may be that the existing sales force is not capable of covering effectively the potential market demand. Wholesale distribution should be considered to cater for the demands of a rapidly changing marketplace. The increased use of existing outlets may not reflect the changes in demand; for example, younger fashion-conscious women, and it may be necessary to amend the distribution channels accordingly.
   3.3 More to the point, products must be modified in order to conform to the requirements of these new channel members. Product research will identify customer needs and changing patterns of buyer behaviour. Clearly, there is a need to understand the motives of the potential customer and to ignore this purely product-driven orientation. If there is sufficient evidence to suggest that products should be modified in order to meet customer demand, then it should be done.
   3.4 Clearly, sales force attitudes need to be considered. The effective use of sales targets/quotas for all products should increase the sales performance. It may be that specialist salespeople are employed/retrained to service new accounts and new channel members.

Conclusions

Clearly, Allwarm is currently very sales-product-oriented and it cannot continue in this vein. It must reassess its objectives and future strategies with marketing very much in mind. It must determine:

(a) Is the product mix adequate for the changing marketplace?

(*b*) How is the marketplace changing? Is it moving away from high-quality natural fibres and yarns?

(*c*) Is there a defined market segment for the product or is the market more diverse?

(*d*) What new products should be developed?

(*e*) Are the existing distribution channels effective and, if not, which new channels need to be considered?

The company would be well advised to approach its business with marketing in mind and to be aware of customers' needs. A wider product range with wider distribution channels is vital if the company is to continue to expand and not to be overtaken by events.

Notes on approach/answer

Here we can see a slightly different 'house style' in answering by our hypothetical candidate. You can see, however, that the elements of the approach – the use of clear section headings, a clear focus on the questions, an emphasis on action and a professional style – are all still in evidence.

★ ★ ★ ★ ★

We shall now look at our final worked example of a mini-case from the CIM's examinations, this time from the Advanced Certificate level Marketing Operations.

ADVANCED CERTIFICATE IN MARKETING
MARKETING OPERATIONS

Walkers 'Fantasy'

In 1994, with 87 retail stores nationwide and a turnover of £38 million, Walkers jewellers could claim a 7 per cent share of the high street jewellery market. They faced severe competition from several multiple jewellery retailers, such as H. Samuel, and a large number of independent stores.

The Walkers chain has been built through a series of acquisitions which still trade under their separate identities.

In recent months the sale of gold jewellery within Walkers has been in decline, and now accounts for 24 per cent of sales turnover against a previous five-year moving average of 33 per cent. Yet diamonds and watches have retained their sales percentage at 29 per cent and 24 per cent respectively.

National sales are down on last year by 4.5 per cent and return on capital employed down by 20 per cent on a five-year average percentage of 13.75 per cent.

Just nine months ago Walkers introduced a high-margin, most appealing branded range of coordinated gold jewellery, 'Fantasy', which today constitutes 188 pieces distributed nationally.

Apart from the large multiples, media advertising is hitherto unknown for jewellery items, especially gold, and normally tactical press advertising is used.

The newly appointed marketing manager has the task of arresting this decline in gold sales and projecting the Fantasy range to restore profitability.

In your capacity as the newly appointed marketing manager you are required to give a preliminary assessment of the position by answering the questions below.

Question

(a) List the strengths, weaknesses, opportunities and threats facing Walkers. **(25 marks)**
(b) Make short-term operational proposals to build sales of the 'Fantasy' range of coordinated gold jewellery with a promotional budget limited to 6 per cent of projected sales. **(25 marks)**

★ ★ ★ ★ ★

Approach

Here are the key pointers in the case and questions which our candidate should have taken into account:

1   The role is that of newly appointed marketing manager required to make a *preliminary* assessment of the position. The word 'preliminary' is crucial, as it emphasizes the fact that this is only the first step in what is likely to be a more wide-ranging and complex process.

2   A straightforward SWOT analysis is required for part (*a*) of this question. Although, as usual, there is little detailed information in the case, it is important not to be too general in approach by simply listing the SWOT factors. The possible SWOT factors must be those that are specifically relevant to the market and company described in the case.

3   In part (*b*) the key pointers are the references to '*short-term operational*' proposals and restrictions on the budget. The examiner would have been looking to use the budget effectively and creatively. Obviously a promotional campaign is called for, but this probably needs to be planned with a central theme in mind. The emphasis on the 'short term' should not detract from the long-term position of the company.

Answer

Report on SWOT analysis and proposals for the short-term future: Walkers Jewellers

(*a*)   *Strengths, weaknesses, opportunities and threats*

1   Introduction

As the newly appointed marketing manager I have conducted an internal investigation to pinpoint Walkers' major strengths and weaknesses. Furthermore, this is followed by an analysis of the opportunities and threats facing the company. The second part of the report contains operational proposals to build short-term sales of the 'Fantasy' range of gold jewellery.

2   Strengths

- Perhaps our greatest strength is that, despite recent difficulties, we are still well established in the high street jewellery market in that our name is known to the public.
- We have a nationwide retail network with outlets in every major town and city in Great Britain.
- Our diamond jewellery and watch division have retained their turnover percentages at 29 per cent and 24 per cent respectively over the past five years and are both strong product categories.
- The introduction of the 'Fantasy' range into our business portfolio nine months ago. This range is branded, which will help promote our corporate identity. It is also a high-margin product which should help to solve some of the financial difficulties which face us at present.
- Test marketing and sales to date indicate a favourable response to this most appealing range of jewellery. As the range constitutes such a wide variety of pieces there are items to suit every budget and most tastes.

- Although sales are down 4.5 per cent on last year, we still have a high sales turnover and command a reasonable share of the high street jewellery market. (This evaluation is based upon the assumption that last year's sales turnover and market share, which are not given in the case study, are roughly equivalent in inflation-adjusted terms to the 1994 figures of £38 million and 3 per cent. I am making this assumption as no evidence is given to the contrary!)

3 Weaknesses

- Walkers has grown through the acquisition of a number of outlets which still trade under their original names. I strongly believe that this is a mistake, and that all our outlets should come under the Walkers name to extend consumer awareness of our company and produce a stronger, more unified image to the public.
- The sale of gold jewellery has been declining in relation to our other products and now only accounts for 24 per cent of sales turnover as opposed to 33 per cent in previous years.
- Financially our performance has worsened in the past twelve months. In the last fiscal year sales have fallen by 4.5 per cent and ROCE is down by 20 per cent on a five-year average of 13.75 per cent.

4 Threats

- The country is still coming out of a recession, and unfortunately the luxury goods market, into which category we as jewellers fall, has been severely hit. At a time when many families have lost their homes, and businesses have been declared bankrupt, jewellery purchases have not been a priority for most people.
- We face severe competitive pressure from other jewellery retailers, such as Ratners, H. Samuel, the Jewellers Guild and numerous independent outlets.
- Recent years have seen an increasing proportion of disposable income being spent on non-retail goods such as holidays and leisure activities.
- We also face extended rivalry from industries and organizations producing substitute retail products such as quality clothing, video and stereo goods, and so on.

5 Opportunities

- Despite the seemingly bleak environment in which we currently find ourselves I have identified a number of opportunities available to us.
- We have seen the abandonment of all trade barriers within the European Community. This has given us the chance to market our products to the world's largest single market; an opportunity of which we should now endeavour to take full advantage.
- Approximately 40 per cent of the UK's population now falls within the 30–40 age bracket. This represents a lucrative market, and I have proposed that a fuller investigation be made regarding the needs and wants of this age range.
- Movements in the economy are cyclical, and the past recession will be

followed (hopefully soon) by a boom, which historically means increased expenditure in the gold jewellery market.

- Traditionally media advertising is not used by retailers of gold jewellery. This form of media communication could represent a potent marketing tool for Walkers.

(*b*) *Short-term tactical proposals to build sales of the 'Fantasy' range of coordinated gold jewellery with a promotional budget limited to 6 per cent of projected sales*

1 Key considerations in operational plans

With a fairly tight budget due to our current financial difficulties, it is essential that this budget be used effectively and creatively. There are numerous promotional tools available to us in order to boost our gold jewellery sales in general and, in particular, to promote our new range of jewellery, 'Fantasy'.

First, I would like to point-out the importance of this promotional campaign being a coordinated one. A common theme *must* be central to each method of communication used in order to project one simple but powerful message.

After discussions with an advertising agency a rough brief has been worked upon, the central theme of which is that our jewellery, particularly 'Fantasy' are collectable items that may be added to at various times until the consumer has built up her own set. The quality and design of the new range will obviously be an integral part of our campaign.

2 Advertising

Although I realize that television advertising is not a medium normally associated with our product, I believe it represents a golden opportunity for 'Fantasy'. We face a great deal of competition in the high street from numerous outlets all selling roughly the same products. Consumers are not normally loyal to a particular retailer of jewellery; the purchase of gold jewellery is a high involvement purchase, but people in our market are not concerned about where they buy it from.

This lack of loyalty towards any one outlet means that consumers are very susceptible to above-the-line advertising, particularly a form as powerful as television. If we can raise awareness of our new product among consumer groups, we will have gained a strong competitive edge over our leading rivals.

Furthermore, to save money, which is scarce at the moment, I propose a 'burst' strategy – that is, advertising only at certain times of the year when consumers are more likely to purchase gold jewellery, i.e. around Christmas, Valentine's Day, the summer months, which see the greatest amount of wedding anniversaries, etc. This could be backed up by our more usual forms of advertising in the press and on billboards.

I also propose that we make greater use of direct marketing. We have at our disposal an extensive customer databank due to the credit facilities we offer. This should be used to identify the most lucrative customers, who should be made aware of our new 'Fantasy' range in this manner. Direct marketing is a cheap and effective way to target customer groups with specific messages.

3 Sales promotion

I suggest that attractive window displays be used to draw people into our stores. Similarly, bold point-of-purchase displays can be used to great effect. This type of sales promotion is generally cost-effective and may be used nationwide initially. The details concerning the type of displays to be used will be worked out shortly.

4 Personal selling

A professional and dedicated sales force is one of the most powerful tools any retailer can have. Sales people are in direct contact with the public, and their skills in negotiating a sale and customer core can ultimately mean the difference between profit and loss in each outlet.

I propose that a brief be sent to each branch of Walkers where the 'Fantasy' range is sold instructing the sales staff to heavily promote the new jewellery items. An incentive scheme is presently being drawn up offering bonus cash and other prizes to the sales people who achieve the highest sales figures.

★ ★ ★ ★ ★

Summary

This then completes our sample of worked cases together with specimen answers. In the final two chapters of Part One we show you first how to present your answers in report-type format and finally how to avoid the most common mistakes which candidates make on mini-cases.

5 *Writing reports for mini-case studies*

Up to now it has been stressed that your answers should normally be in report format. You will also note from the worked examples of mini-case answers that the precise format of a report – introductions, numbering systems, use of subheadings and so on – can vary. Reports differ in length, degree of formality and format as much as they do in content. For example, in practice some reports are very short and informal, perhaps presented as a memorandum; others (although not for the mini-cases) will run into thousands of words.

However, all reports have common elements and benefit from adherence to a number of simple rules in their preparation. The most important of these elements and rules are as follows:

1 Planning the report

The planning stage starts with:

- The purpose of the report.
- What is to be included.
- How it is to be presented.
- To whom it is to be presented.

At this planning stage in the actual examination the questions should be broken down into their component parts and a structure designed to ensure that each of these parts is covered in the report and that the *examiner can see that they have been covered*. Sectionalization of the report and the use of clear headings (for each separate question) will help to achieve this, but so too will starting the report with a statement of terms of reference.

2 Terms of reference

At the start of a report it is a good idea to write out the terms of reference so that you can demonstrate that you understand precisely what you have been asked to do. Terms of reference should include the following:

2.1 Who the report is for and/or by whom it has been requested. *Example*: 'At the request of the marketing manager of Bloggs plc.'
2.2 The areas to be covered (i.e. the questions). *Example*:

- Methods of entry into overseas markets.

- The promotional mix.
- Pricing strategies.

2.3 The intended outcome of the report. *Example*:

- To establish strategies for developing export markets.
- To make proposals for a coordinated promotional campaign.

2.4 The constraints/assumptions (if any) which affect the report. *Example*:

- Within a proposed budget for promotion of £100,000
  or
- In compiling the report it has been assumed that the rate of inflation will continue to be 3 per cent per annum.

3 Proposals and recommendations

Remember, reports are not extended essays but concise statements which set out our thoughts simply and clearly.

In most reports, and the mini-cases are no exception, it is the proposals and recommendations which are of prime interest (although clearly these must be based on sound analysis).

All proposals and recommendations should be justified, but do not bore the reader with over-complicated or in-depth analysis. For the most part, in the mini-cases, any detailed calculations and analysis, if required in the report, should form part of the appendices.

4 Structuring a report

As we have noted, the conventions for structuring a report vary considerably. Here is one example of a report structure which you could use in the examinations.

4.1 *Title page*:
Title of report, to whom addressed, the date, author's name and company.

4.2 *Terms of reference*:
Resumé of terms of reference (as above).

4.3 *Contents list*:
Report structure together with the numbering system which is used throughout the report. Major headings and subheadings would be shown indexed by page.

4.4 *The main report*:
This should include the detailed facts and recommendations contained in the report.

4.5 *Appendices*:
So that the main flow of argument is not interrupted by a mass of detail, financial and other data can be summarized or referred to in the report but attached at the end. As an alternative you could insert a *summary* of your main findings and recommendations between the title page and terms of reference. This is quite common and useful in report writing.

Above all, it is important that you structure your report to achieve the following:

- The report should, as far as is possible, be interesting. Remember, the examiner will have to read dozens of these reports.
- The report should be easy to understand.
- The report should follow a logical sequence leading the reader along a particular path.

5 Presentation

Presentation is crucial for a report to be well received. Each page must be well laid out to appeal to the reader's eye.

The use of white space, headings and subheadings, indentations and report numbering systems should be applied to create maximum impact.

You do not have much time in the mini-case examination, but in any event a report should contain short, sharp sections and paragraphs.

In short, write simply, write briefly, write positively and avoid cluttering the main body of your report with elaborate diagrams, calculations and charts and tables.

6 Mini-case failure – how to minimize it

Much of what is said in this chapter is basically a reiteration of what has been said already. It must therefore be viewed more as a summary or reinforcement.

We provide advice on examination tactics and timing and then go on to discuss balance, volume, structure presentation and style. Finally, we offer advice on answering the question set, and not what you would like to answer – a common cause of failure!

Tactics

Decide *before* going into the examination room whether to attempt the mini-case as Part A of the paper first or not.

To help you settle in the examination room and to build your confidence it may be wise to handle the mini-case second and devote the first one and a half hours of the three-hour paper to answering Part B questions. However, it is not our aim to prescribe what you should do: adopt the method with which you feel most comfortable.

Timing

Spend *only* one and a half hours on the diploma and advanced certificate mini-cases and one hour or so on the certificate mini-cases.

Budget your time to allow time to read, time to write and time to read over. Try to avoid the race against the clock to complete the question paper.

Where there is a differential allocation of marks allocate your time accordingly.

Time yourself carefully.

Balance

Aim to produce a balanced paper with appropriate attention given to all parts of the question paper. Balance your time and your effort to gain best results.

Volume

Aim to produce an answer script of substance. Substance scores points, but avoid the tendency to waffle.

Structure

Develop structural answers and use well conceived headings which follow a logical sequence.

Presentation

Remember, packaging sells the product!

Clear layout and good presentation will increase the appeal of your answer.

Use the page to full advantage – leave gaps, create white space, underline, box out key points – these will improve the impact of your answer. Even the most illegible handwriting can be improved using these techniques to create interest on the page.

Style

Adopt report format at all times. This leads to a succinct approach with practice and enables more ideas to be covered within the time limits of the examination.

Answer the questions set

Above all, the examiner is looking for an answer to the *actual* questions that have been set.

Do not superimpose pre-planned structures unless they are appropriate to the actual questions asked. Do not use marketing plans, market entry plans, sales plans, marketing communications plans, SWOT analysis, *unless these are asked for in the question.*

Answers should be tailor-made to fit the case study scenario. They should relate to the issues raised and not be remote from the situation in hand.

Answer the mini-case questions as a practitioner, not as a student of marketing.

Do not depend upon textbook material to produce academic answers. Focus your attention upon producing real world answers to the real problems with which you are faced.

Where necessary, quantify your answers to ensure that your recommendations for action are not based purely upon a qualitative assessment of the situation in hand. Remember that most marketing decisions have time and cost implications.

Often you are given a role – a marketing consultant, account executive, line marketing manager or whatever. *Use this role* to answer the questions – it will help you to produce reasoned judgements and maybe even to aspire to the difficulties of implementation.

If in a role you are required to make recommendations, remember who is to do what, where, when and how and remember the rationale for it – why.

Recommendations should be supported with appropriate justification. Never leave the question 'why?' open to the examiner.

Make sure that your recommendations are within the resource capabilities of the organization(s) concerned. This means that there is a need for a realistic assessment of the company and market constraints. This may prove difficult. Therefore it is suggested that you make relevant assumptions before producing recommendations for courses of action.

Remember that many case study scenarios and the questions asked of them involve change. Change involves people and therefore the organizational implications of your recommendations should not be overlooked. Change also has time and cost considerations. Do not overlook these.

Do not assume that all courses of action will work to achieve the stated purpose or objectives. Propose contingency actions!

Questions for the CIM examinations are rarely simplistic. Each has a set of dimensions designed to achieve objectives. Therefore you must read, read over again, then read over slowly and carefully the *actual* questions to determine the actual requirements. Then structure your answers to meet with these requirements. It is wise therefore to make assumptions before answering the question to ensure that you are on the same wavelength as the person who will assess your script. When structuring your answers make sure that your structure covers all parts of the questions set. Do not try to skirt around the real issues of the examination questions.

Remember, marks are awarded for answers, not analysis. Do not waste time on analysis at the cost of not putting enough time and effort into answering the questions set.

Part Two   Mini-cases – Examples and Answers

7 *Introduction to Part Two*

By now you should have a good grasp of the nature of mini-cases and how to tackle them. We have looked at the background to the development of the mini-cases and their structure. We have also introduced you to a framework for analysing them and shown, through a series of sample cases and worked examples, how a well prepared candidate might tackle the mini-cases. However, the only effective way to prepare yourself for the mini-case examinations is through practice. In Part Two of the text, therefore, we have selected a range of mini-cases for you to work on.

Chapter 8 is comprised of Certificate level subject mini-cases. As mentioned in Part One, many of these are actually mini-mini-cases and are generally shorter than those selected from the Diploma level. We have also included a couple of examples of Certificate level papers where stimulus material has been used instead of an actual case study. Remember, these are somewhat different from true mini-cases but, as mentioned earlier, the general approach to mini-cases is still broadly relevant.

Chapter 9 contains the more conventional mini-cases used for the Diploma level subjects. As we have already pointed out, these cases are for you to practise on under self-imposed examination conditions. Our instructions on how to use these cases is contained in Chapter 1, section 1.3. You should now remind yourself of these instructions.

Chapters 10 and 11 contain the specimen answers to the selected case studies for the Certificate/Advanced Certificate and Diploma level cases respectively. Remember, do not read the specimen answers to the cases before you have at least made some attempt to tackle them on your own.

When you go through the specimen answers do not be put off if you have not written as much as in some of these answers. Remember, these are supposed to represent the ideal comprehensive answer. What you should look for when you read the specimen answers is structure and whether or not your answer has followed a similar structure.

8 Certificate level: selected mini-cases

This chapter contains a selection of mini-cases together with examples of 'stimulus-type' material for the Certificate and Advanced Certificate level subjects. The cases, together with the subject and level which each case examines, are shown below.

In the case of stimulus material-type cases we have indicated the nature of the stimulus material by referring to it in the title or topic. So, for example, Case 8.5 uses stimulus material based on a newspaper article.

Case	Title/Topic	Level	Subject
8.1	Fine Furnishings Ltd	Certificate	Marketing Fundamentals
8.2	Dairy Slim	Certificate	Business Communications
8.3	PME Ltd	Certificate	Fundamentals of Selling
8.4	Textbook quotes *	Certificate	Understanding Customers
8.5	Newspaper articles *	Certificate	Selling Environment
8.6	After Eight	Advanced Certificate	Promotional Practice
8.7	Bishop Business Publishing Ltd	Advanced Certificate	Management Information for Marketing and Sales
8.8	The Garden Design and Landscape Co.	Advanced Certificate	Effective Management for Marketing
8.9	IKEA Furniture Retailer	Advanced Certificate	Marketing Operations
8.10	Chicago Mutual	Advanced Certificate	Effective Management for Sales
8.11	Homeclean Limited	Advanced Certificate	Sales Operations

* Denotes stimulus material.

Remember to work through each case on your own first and prepare your own answer before comparing your answer with the specimen one shown in Chapter 10.

CERTIFICATE IN MARKETING
MARKETING FUNDAMENTALS

Time: $1\frac{1}{4}$ hours
Total: 40 marks

Case 8.1 : Fine Furnishings Limited

Fine Furnishings Limited is a small chain of distributors of good-quality office furniture, carpets, safes and filing cabinets. The company keeps in touch with advances made in the office furniture field worldwide and introduces those products which are in keeping with the needs of the market in terms of design, workmanship, value for money and technical specifications.

It is contended that furniture purchased is a capital investment, and a wise decision can help the buyer save on future expenses, because cheaper alternatives have to be replaced more frequently.

Fine Furnishings trades only in good-quality furniture which is sturdily constructed. Differences between its products and cheaper, lower quality ones are well known to those who have several years of experience in the business.

An important feature, the company feels, is the availability of a complete list of components of the furniture system. This enables customers to add bits and pieces of matching design and colour in the future. Such components are available for sale separately. Systems are maintained in stock by the company for a number of years, and spare parts for chairs and other furniture are always available.

The company has experienced a downturn in trade over the past two years. In addition, it had to trim its profit margins. Last year, it barely broke even and this year it is heading for a small loss for the first time in the company's twenty-year history.

Question

(a) Advise the company in relation to its product mix. How will your recommendation affect the company's image?   **(13 marks)**
(b) Advise the company in relation to its stockholding policy. How will your recommendations affect customer service?   **(13 marks)**
(c) Suggest ways in which promotional activity might help the company out of the difficulties it now faces.   **(14 marks)**

★   ★   ★   ★   ★

CERTIFICATE IN MARKETING
BUSINESS COMMUNICATIONS

Time: 1¼ hours
Total: 40 marks

Case 8.2: Dairy Slim

Question

You are marketing manager for a company which specializes in producing dairy products for the 'slimming market'. The results of your latest research have just been published (see below) and you have been asked to:

(a) Write a short formal report to the marketing director, Mr David Forsythe, highlighting the conclusions drawn from this research. Your recommendations will be used to help identify new products for possible development in this market. **(30 marks)**
(b) Choose an appropriate method for graphical presentation of each of the categories of research information provided and use it to present this data more effectively. **(10 marks)**

Market research results

This research was carried out from January to June 1995, using in-depth interviews in the respondents' homes, recorded on tape and interpreted by ourselves, 'The XYZ Research Agency', specialists in market research for the food industry.

Sample size: 500   Age range: 15–55
Socio-economic groups: ABC1 *   Locations: Bristol, Manchester and
                                 Greater London
Sex: Males and females

Three broad categories were tested and the results are as follows:

* Socio-economic groupings:

A Higher managerial, chief executives, etc.
B Managerial, executives, etc.
C1 Higher clerical, supervisory, etc.

Motives for wanting to lose weight	*% of respondents mentioning weight problems*
To feel physically good	68
For health reasons	67
To stay fit	43
Because I want to live longer	25
To stay mentally alert	23
To be more attractive	21
To be more popular	15
Methods for weight control	
Avoid certain foods, eat 'slimming items'	32
Eat and drink less	23
Play sports, keep fit	22
Have certain 'diet days'	7
Take medicines, stimulants	3
Foods which people dislike giving up	
Cakes, pies, bakery products	31
Sweets, sugar	23
Beer, alcoholic beverages	17
Meat, sausages, etc.	15
Chocolate	13
Cream	9
Fruit juices	9
Potatoes	9
Pasta	9

In general, the comments also revealed that dieting means a loss of pleasure at mealtimes, causes problems when one can't eat the same as the rest of the family and also one is regarded as being 'ill' when dieting.

* * * * *

CERTIFICATE IN MARKETING
FUNDAMENTALS OF SELLING

Time: $1\frac{1}{4}$ hours
Total: 40 marks

Case 8.3: PME Ltd

PME Ltd has obtained the rights to sell in the UK a range of production line monitoring equipment. These products are different from the company's normal line of business, but existing customers should find them attractive. A typical item of the new equipment has a selling price in the order of £3000, whereas the company's existing product range consists of small ticket items such as micro-switches and consumables selling at little more than £5 to £10.

Another major difference is that the company has won UK-wide distribution rights, whereas until now it has operated on a local scale, supplying industry mainly in the north-west of England. The sales director has representatives who are prepared to move to new territories, and a plan for direct selling of the new product range has been drawn up.

There is within the sales department an experienced telesales department comprising a telesales manager and four telesales staff. This department has for some time complemented the work of the representatives by producing a steady supply of follow-up orders after the representative has opened a new account.

It is the sales director's intention to use similar procedures and techniques with the new products in the new areas.

Question

(a) If you were the telesales manager, what would your reaction be to the sales director's plans? Write a memo to the sales director offering constructive advice. **(14 marks)**

(b) What difficulties would face the representatives who have been assigned to the new product range? **(13 marks)**

(c) It will be vital for the salespeople remote from head office to keep the company informed. Draft a call report form with appropriate headings and indicative content. **(13 marks)**

Time: $1\frac{1}{4}$ hours
Total: 40 marks

Case 8.4: 'Textbook quotes'

Quotation 1 (from Michael Hammer and James Champy: *Re-Engineering the Corporation – a Manifesto for Business Revolution*, London: Nicholas Brearley, 1993).

Since the early 1980s, in the United States and other developed countries, the dominant force in the seller–customer relationship has shifted. Sellers no longer have the upper hand; customers do. Customers now tell suppliers what they want, when they want it, how they want it, and what they will pay. This new situation is unsettling to companies that have known life only in the mass market.

In reality, a mass market never existed, but for most of this century the *idea* of the mass market provided manufacturers and service providers – from Henry Ford's car company to Thomas Watson's computer company – with the useful fiction that their customers were more or less alike . . .

Now that they have choices, though, customers no longer behave as if they are all cast in the same mould, Customers – consumers and corporations alike – demand products and services designed for their unique and particular needs. There is no longer any such notion as *the* customer; there is only *this* customer, the one with whom a seller is dealing at the moment and who now has the capacity to indulge his or her own personal tastes. The mass market has broken into pieces, some as small as a single customer.

Quotation 2 (from B. Joseph Pine II: *Mass Customization – The New Frontier in Business Competition*, Harvard Business School Press, 1993).

People do not like hard-sell tactics, but they will tolerate them to acquire something they really want. If what they purchase turns out to be not *quite* what they wanted, their dissatisfaction with the product is magnified by their dissatisfaction with the sales tactics.

The basic problem (in years gone by) was that the focus of the marketing function of mass producers was not on *marketing* – it was on *selling*, on 'pushing product'. Selling is a necessary part of the marketing function, but marketing is so much more, as management guru Peter Drucker observes:

'There will always, one can assume, be need for some selling. But the aim of marketing is to make selling superfluous. The aim of marketing is to know and understand the customer so well that the product or service fits him and sells itself. Ideally, marketing should result in a customer who is ready to buy. All that should be needed then is to make the product or service available.'

Question

(*a*) Market segmentation is based on the proposition that customers can be categorized according to their typical wants, needs and expectations. What is the future of segmentation, given the views of Hammer and Champy?   (**13 marks**)

(*b*) Even if Drucker is right in claiming that the aim of marketing is to make selling superfluous, what are the practical problems associated with 'knowing and understanding the customer so well that the product or service . . . sells itself'?   (**13 marks**)

(*c*) To what extent do the arguments advanced in both quotations apply to any one of the following marketing environments:

  • the public sector (government departments and authorities responsible for the administration of local/municipal affairs)
  • the third sector, i.e. voluntary or charitable organizations
  • the marketing of services to internal customers within organizations.

Note that you should only write about *any one* of these three options.
                                                                    (**14 marks**)

★   ★   ★   ★   ★

CERTIFICATE IN SELLING
SELLING ENVIRONMENT

Time: $1\frac{1}{4}$ hours
Total: 40 marks

Case 8.5: Newspaper articles: Paints and the environment

Paint protects much of the modern world against the environment and adds colour to life, but is it itself an environmental problem? Paint makers have already responded, but eco-friendlier coatings are not always better – and their cost may be more than buyers will be willing to pay.

Four years ago there was palpable fear at the industry's conferences about what tighter environmental controls were going to do to profitability and, in some cases, survival. It is not that the industry is full of companies bent on profit at the cost of pollution. Rather, its most reputable members have spent millions on compliance with new laws and in developing new and greener products.

They are now looking for compromise in an age of politicized environmentalism, when the goalposts have tended to be moved further away as industry has achieved the new standards demanded of it.

The main pollution issue for the industry is the emission of volatile organic compounds (VOCs) when the solvents used in paint evaporate. The paint industry's response has been to develop water-based coatings or put more solids – pigments and resins – in the formulation.

Except for decorative emulsions used indoors on walls and ceilings, 'water-based' does not necessarily mean 'VOC-free' – 'green equals reduction, rather than elimination'.

Source: *Financial Times* survey, April 1994.

Question

(a) Using examples, outline the issues facing a paint maker squeezed between two laws:
  (i) the law of the land which imposes ever stricter environmental controls **(15 marks)**
  (ii) the law of supply and demand. **(15 marks)**
(b) Suggest the main internal and external sources of data an industrial paint maker might use to identify sales trends over the past five years.
(10 marks)

★   ★   ★   ★   ★

ADVANCED CERTIFICATE IN MARKETING
ADVANCED CERTIFICATE IN SALES MANAGEMENT
PROMOTIONAL PRACTICE

Time: $1\frac{1}{2}$ hours
Total: 50 marks

Case 8.6: After Eight

In this case you are asked to play the role of the account manager at J. Walter Thompson, the London-based advertising agency holding the After Eight account. You will be considering the development of an advertising campaign to support a line extension within the After Eight range.

Rowntree Mackintosh, producers of the After Eight, are ranked as the third largest producers of confectionery globally, with a turnover of over £60m from 83 countries. Rowntree Mackintosh, part of Nestlé, has its headquarters in York, England.

Confectionery represents approximately 75 per cent of Rowntree Mackintosh's total sales by value. The products produced by the company include Kit-Kat, Black Magic, Smarties, Quality Street and After Eight.

After Eight was launched in Britain during the 1960s after Rowntree Mackintosh identified a gap in the market for expensive, exclusive, boxed chocolates. The agency selected to work on the account was J. Walter Thompson based in London. The agency suggested the name 'After Eight' and produced the pack design, using a distinctive logo and packaging design in which the chocolates were presented within individual envelopes.

The brand was positioned as a uniquely presented, wafer-thin, high-quality mint chocolate which should be enjoyed after a relaxed dinner or other comparable occasion. After Eight should be associated with the elegance, sophistication and social status of a good hostess and her guests. As an affordable token of friendship or appreciation, After Eight reflects the good taste of the giver and will flatter the receiver.

Test-marketed initially in Scotland and supported by press advertising, the product was then rolled out nationally. However, a sales breakthrough was achieved when TV advertising was used within the Yorkshire TV region, resulting in a 64 per cent increase in sales.

The 1970s saw the successful launch of the product across Europe. The basic advertising proposition was unchanged, but allowances were made for the variations of culture.

In order to preserve the brand identity within creative executions, a set of 'Advertising Guidelines' were generated, detailing the appropriate methods to portray the right life styles. This system was put in place in order to ensure the proper implementation of agreed policies and actions and to combat disruption caused by the changes of staff at both Rowntree Mackintosh and the agency.

Following the international success of After Eight, Rowntree Mackintosh has launched in the UK a new 5-pack intended to be an indulgence snack competing with the countline line sector. A new national campaign is to be supported by a £1m media budget.

Question

As the account manager at J. Walter Thompson, you are required to write proposals in an outline report for the launch of the 5-pack within the UK. In particular your report should include the following:

(a) Details of the potential target market for the 5-pack.   **(15 marks)**
(b) Recommendations on the inter-media selection and scheduling.
                                                                (20 marks)
(c) Guidelines on how public relations activities can be used to support the media campaign.   **(15 marks)**

★   ★   ★   ★   ★

ADVANCED CERTIFICATE IN MARKETING
ADVANCED CERTIFICATE IN SALES MANAGEMENT
MANAGEMENT INFORMATION FOR
MARKETING AND SALES

Time: 1½ hours
Total: 50 marks

Case 8.7: *Bishop Business Publishing Ltd*

Bishop Business Publishing Ltd sells business books through three main distribution channels which are:

- Wholesale
- Retail
- Direct sales to customers.

The company is considering investing heavily in new technology and focusing its efforts on direct sales since these appear to be more profitable because no trade discounts need to be given. Wholesale customers receive 50 per cent trade discount and retailers receive an average 35 per cent trade discount. It is customary in the trade not to charge carriage/delivery charges to wholesale and retail customers. Direct sales customers pay a nominal charge of £2 on a single book order and 10 per cent of the order value for multiple orders. The average non-discounted price of books published by Bishop is £15 per title.

Current cost structure for a single book via each distribution channel

	Wholesale £	Retail £	Direct £
Selling price	15.00	15.00	15.00
Trade discount	(7.50)	(5.25)	NIL
Net receipt	7.50	9.75	15.00
Direct production costs	(3.00)	(3.00)	(3.00)
Author royalty (1)	(0.75)	(0.97)	(1.50)
Promotion (2)	(0.50)	(0.50)	(1.00)
Distribution/Carriage (3)	(0.50)	(2.00)	(2.00)
Net profit	2.75	3.28	7.50

1 Author royalty payments are 10 per cent of the net receipt figure.
2 Promotional costs per title tend to average about 50p for providing trade catalogues and trade mailings which are currently handled in-house.

Promotion to direct customers is via mailings containing flyers for customers to respond directly to make a purchase. The mailing lists are rented from specialist database marketing firms who charge an average of 10p per name (label).

3 Distribution costs are averaged and reflect costs per average order size. Wholesalers tend to order in batches of 100, whereas retailers tend to order in units of four and direct customers tend to order single copies.

The volume of business expressed as a percentage of total sales turnover is currently:

	%
Wholesale	30
Retail	50
Direct	20
	100

Question

Your answer should be presented in report format which addresses the key issues. Any appropriate calculations you think necessary to justify your recommendations should be contained within the body of the report.

(a) Using the information provided, suggest possible courses of action for Bishop Business Publishing Ltd.   **(17 marks)**

(b) What further quantitative and qualitative information should the company obtain before taking any decision to eliminate particular channels of distribution?   **(17 marks)**

(c) Explain how technology might be employed to assist the company in future.   **(16 marks)**

★   ★   ★   ★   ★

ADVANCED CERTIFICATE IN MARKETING
EFFECTIVE MANAGEMENT FOR MARKETING

Time: $1\frac{1}{2}$ hours
Total: 50 marks

Case 8.8: The Garden Design and Landscape Company

The mid-1990s have been tough for businesses of all sizes. Markets have been increasingly competitive and demand sluggish. Survival has been the goal of many, and the need to get the best out of all available resources paramount to that goal being successfully achieved.

The Garden Design and Landscape Company is one such organization. It has survived for over eighteen years and has a turnover of some £2.5 million, with about £1 million from household contracts, new drives, patios and garden layouts. The balance comes from a mixture of public sector and corporate work, mainly maintenance contracts but with some new project work. Sales revenue has fallen slightly over the last few years, but has declined in real terms by over 15 per cent since 1992. Average order values have fallen and so has the operating profit.

Based in the south-east of England the company has three centres, each with a small sales office and showroom. There are currently some 120 full-time staff, but a number of casual workers are employed as necessary to meet the seasonal shifts in workload. Staff numbers have fallen from 160 in 1992.

Having attended a recent seminar which examined the value of a strategic marketing approach to planning, the managing director approached you to act as a consultant and undertake an objective review of the current position of the business and to make recommendations for the changes which might be necessary if the company is to be ready to meet the challenges of the rest of the 1990s and improve the overall financial performance of the business.

You have completed your initial audits and the following summarizes some of your key findings:

- The business is operationally product-oriented.
- There is little use of available information and no real information system.
- Planning is *ad hoc* and its value not really understood.
- The organization is hierarchical in structure with no real incentives for the individual work teams.
- Absenteeism is high, averaging over 1.5 days per month per manual worker.
- There is a small field sales team of a sales manager and four sales staff and six full-time administrative support staff. There is also a Marketing

Manager who is mainly responsible for sales literature and advertising and reports directly to the managing director.

- There is increased competition and the market is increasingly price-competitive.
- There are no clear links between sales and marketing and little coordination of effort between the sales teams in the three centres.
- Enquiries generated are high, but the conversion from sales visits to orders is low, only 1 in 7; in the past it has been as high as 1 in 3.
- Only the most basic customer records are maintained.

Question

(*a*) Bearing in mind that any available budget for change will be limited, what proposals would you make to help the firm change to a more market-oriented culture? Provide an indication of the time scale and likely costs for your recommendations. **(35 marks)**

(*b*) Briefly outline what actions you would recommend to improve the effectiveness of the marketing and sales team. **(15 marks)**

★　★　★　★　★

ADVANCED CERTIFICATE IN SALES MANAGEMENT
EFFECTIVE MANAGEMENT FOR SALES

Time: 1½ hours
Total: 50 marks

Case 8.10: Chicago Mutual

Although the company's roots can be traced back to the United States in the 1920s, Chicago Mutual have only been trading in the UK since 1993. Most insurance companies tend to cover a broad spectrum of insurance services like automobile, fire, life, etc. Chicago Mutual concentrates on the personal health and personal accident fields.

Its growth can best be measured by the increase in the volumes of premiums collected in a financial year, and some of its annual volumes have been as follows:

	1982	1985	1988	1991	1994	1995
£ million	4.2	14.4	23.2	43.4	49.2	54.8

During this time, the rate of sales of new business has steadily increased, but this was accompanied by a disturbing increase in the cancellations of existing policies.

The task of the sales person is divided into three parts:

1 Gaining new business.
2 Servicing existing policies (i.e., renewing them).
3 Upgrading existing policies (i.e., persuading customers to increase their cover).

The company does not advertise, and rotates its coverage of territories on a six-monthly basis. Thus, customers see a representative only twice a year.

For the sales manager there are persistent problems. Staff turnover is high, with the average length of employment of the sales person being six months. His success, therefore, depends upon having a 'core' of long-serving members in his sales team.

New members of the sales team take some time to become useful and productive employees. Once hired they spend two weeks in a training school to learn the standard sales presentation, how to answer objections and some knowledge of consumer and organizational buying behaviour.

The marketplace primarily consists of shops and other small businesses.

In addition, the more enterprising sales people endeavour to sell to larger businesses and through bank managers, solicitors and accountants. Cold calling on individual homes also features when attempting to find business.

Commission is earned both on sales and upgrades and also by renewing and collecting premiums on existing policies. A problem for the sales manager is in motivating the sales force to spend as much time and energy in gaining new business as the energy they seem to spend in servicing the old.

The sales manager's job in fact depends upon producing an increase in premium volume in each six-monthly cycle. That, in turn, depends upon his ability on a number of fronts:

(*a*) Selecting the right people for training.
(*b*) Early field training in order that sales people can quickly apply what they have learned in training.
(*c*) Retaining a core of successful sales people and motivating them to continue their success.
(*d*) Ensuring that sufficient time is left to go on selling missions with his sales staff, as well as selling on his own account.

Question

(*a*) Advise the sales manager upon Chicago Mutual's commission structure. Does it encourage the retention of good sales people? **(25 marks)**
(*b*) 'The training of sales people should not be limited to their induction into the company, but should be an on-going process.' Discuss this contention in relation to this situation. **(25 marks)**

⋆   ⋆   ⋆   ⋆   ⋆

ADVANCED CERTIFICATE IN SALES MANAGEMENT
SALES OPERATIONS

Time: $1\frac{1}{2}$ hours
Total: 50 marks

Case 8.11: *Homeclean Limited*

This company is based in Lancashire and is part of a major West German conglomerate. Homeclean manufactures a range of consumable cleaning items ranging from household brushes, mops and cleaning cloths together with similar products designed for industrial markets.

The raw material used is principally high-density woven material which has a relatively long lifespan, and the company is generally regarded as being at the 'quality' end of the market for such products. The products are packaged and branded so as to make them stand out from more traditional competing products.

In terms of marketing, both industrial and consumer products are distributed through intermediaries and not direct. The sales force thus sell to distributors for industrial products. Advertising plays a key role in the company's marketing efforts, and products are brand-managed in order to create an element of internal competition.

United Kingdom sales for the past three years have been increasing slowly from £3.6 million in 1993 to £4.1 million in 1994 to £4.7 million in 1995. Advertising spend has been about 5 per cent of sales during this period – 75 per cent of which has been through television campaigns. The remainder has been spent on leaflets, in-store campaigns, trade magazines and the press.

The parent company has made a decision to expand further into the European market and has encouraged Homeclean to open up satellite manufacturing plants. It is concerned that Homeclean choose the right advertising agency for this planned expansion. The parent company uses two agencies in Europe, and at one point it attempted to 'impose' one of these agencies on Homeclean's UK operations. Homeclean resisted, saying that European agencies would not understand the UK market. Now the parent company is using this same argument against Homeclean taking its UK advertising campaign (and UK agency) into Europe.

Question

(*a*) In view of the sales turnover figure, is the company justified in engaging so much in above-the-line advertising? Outline the arguments for shifting the emphasis to more direct selling. **(25 marks)** (*b*) What are the key considerations in Homeclean switching the promotional mix to more direct selling? **(25 marks)**

★   ★   ★   ★   ★

9 *Diploma level: selected mini-cases*

In this chapter the selected mini-cases cover the three Diploma level subjects of Marketing Communication, International Marketing, and Planning and Control.

As indicated earlier, you should work through each case systematically before comparing your own answer with the specimen answer in Chapter 11.

Because we are required to cover only three Diploma level subjects, compared with the much larger number of subjects for the Certificate level, we have been able to include four sample cases for each subject. For your convenience we have grouped the cases by subject area as shown below.

Cases (by subject)

(a) *Marketing communications*

Case	Title
9.1	The Mondex Card, Electronic Wallet
9.2	The Ash Grove Kindergarten
9.3	The Big Cat's on the prowl
9.4	Dennison Aggregates

(b) *International marketing strategy*

Case	Title
9.5	Star Engineering
9.6	Leisureworld Bicycles
9.7	Teesside Electrical
9.8	Giant's Castle Games Ltd

(c) *Strategic marketing management: Planning and control*

Case	Title
9.9	Anderson Marine Construction Ltd
9.10	Watergate Pumps Ltd

DIPLOMA IN MARKETING
MARKETING COMMUNICATIONS STRATEGY

Time: 1½ hours
Total: 50 marks

Case 9.1: The Mondex Card, electronic wallet

National Westminster Bank and Midland Bank could save hundreds of millions of pounds by replacing cash with an electronic wallet. The two have set up a joint venture to begin offering customers a plastic 'smartcard' called Mondex, to be used as a substitute for cash.

The banks have refused to reveal the size of their investment in the service. But estimates put the figure at about £70 million between 1990 and 1995.

Recent figures shows that the cost to the UK's banks of shifting cash to fill dispensing machines is £4.5 billion a year. Electronic purses would dramatically reduce that figure.

The two banks are working with BT, which is adapting payphones to accept the card and is developing a new telephone for use at home so that customers will be able to transfer cash from bank accounts to the cards. Analysts estimate that, if the service is successful, it could add £100 million a year to BT's revenues by the year 2000 as the group expands into home services.

The announcement surprised others in the banking industry, as it came just a day after Visa and Mastercard had announced that they were working to develop a common chip standard for smartcards. John Hutchinson, managing director of Visa UK, described Mondex as 'a very interesting experiment'. He said that similar initiatives were afoot in South Africa, Spain and Denmark. However, he issued a warning: 'We need to make sure that we do not have, like the video world did for a while, three different standards.'

Bert Morris, NatWest's deputy chief executive, said that NatWest had approached Midland to take part in the project because the two banks had worked well together on cash machines and Switch debit cards. Other UK banks may be invited to participate in the scheme at a later stage.

The Mondex card will be tested in 1995 in Swindon, Wiltshire, where all 40000 of the banks' customers will be eligible. The partners hope to win customers over from other banks and to have all 1000 or so retailers in Swindon taking part. If Mondex is successful, it will be rolled out to the banks' 11 million customers nationally a year later.

Mondex is a plastic card which stores a cash value electronically on a chip.

This card can be updated using cash machines or specially adapted telephones. Customers will also be able to increase the values on their cards when they do their shopping, in the same way as they are able to ask for cash back when they use a debit card in a supermarket. An electronic wallet will also be available, enabling customers to store cash for transfer to cards, or to transfer cash from one card to another.

Tim Jones, the senior NatWest executive who conceived the idea in March 1990, predicted that in 10 to 15 years' time, 'the telephone will be the dominant way in which electronic money is withdrawn and deposited'.

NatWest said it would begin approaching banking partners worldwide next year as part of a plan to establish Mondex as a global cash payments system.

The card is designed to be used by children as young as five years old, while the Mondex partners hope that it could be used in the future for such things as paying government benefits.

Source: *The Times*, 9 December 1993.

Question

Acting as a consultant to the National Westminster Bank Consortium, you are asked to write a report recommending a marketing communications strategy for this financial service innovation. In your report you are expected to address the following aspects:

(a) What are the problems that marketing communications strategy must address?   **(10 marks)**
(b) What alternative marketing communication activities can be used to solve those problems?   **(10 marks)**
(c) Make recommendations on a choice of strategy for the Swindon test marketing.   **(10 marks)**
(d) Define the means of measuring the effectiveness of your recommended strategy.   **(10 marks)**
(e) Briefly discuss the implications for a roll-out nationally and internationally.   **(10 marks)**

★ ★ ★ ★ ★

DIPLOMA IN MARKETING
MARKETING COMMUNICATIONS STRATEGY

Time: $1\frac{1}{2}$ hours
Total: 50 marks

Case 9.2: *The Ash Grove Kindergarten*

Striving to fulfil the twin roles of career woman and mother, Mrs Lorna Ash had found it almost impossible to find good-quality childcare in the provincial city where she is manager of a large hotel. A determined person with a highly positive attitude towards working women and a history of willingness to take planned risks in her career, Mrs Ash was sure that her own experience demonstrated an unmet market need. Her career in hotel management had taught her how to promote and deliver a consumer service effectively, and she felt that she could apply it to running a business of nursery provision for children not yet of school age.

The necessary permits were soon obtained, but a business plan had to be submitted to her bank and her house remortgaged before the required finance was raised after six months. There were then delays in the delivery of building materials and fittings, but Ash Grove Kindergarten is at last open for business.

The former warehouse, with a 400-square-metre floor area, is centrally located and has been purpose-redesigned. It has considerable individuality of design, layout and decor, thanks to the fact that Mrs Ash's husband trained as a joiner. The Ash Grove Kindergarten provides a large variety of toys, games, outings and miscellaneous activities for more than 60 children, as well as basic preschool education. The staff consists of a qualified nursery officer, a qualified nursery nurse and five unqualified assistants. Meals can be cooked on the premises. No through traffic passes the entrance and parking is easy.

The target market is middle-class professionals, to whom Ash Grove offers an alternative to the various private nurseries already in existence. Mrs Ash has also wondered about targeting corporate clients. She chose the description 'kindergarten' specifically to differentiate it from the competition and to confer an air of exclusivity.

Mrs Ash's short-term objective is 'to gain the reputation of being a well run, happy place, providing a good level of care and attention to children in its care'. In the longer term, she aims to expand the premises and increase the numbers and to be recognized by everyone as the 'best' nursery in the city.

The profit and loss forecasts prepared for the bank predict an operating loss of £2,500 in year one, followed by net annual profits before tax of £52000 and £60000 in years two and three. Mrs Ash has made a personal investment of £12000 and has a standing overdraft facility of £6,000.

The tariff has been set at £60 per week per child full-time, or £35 for part-time attendance from either 0830 to 1300 or 1330 to 1800. Competitors, apart from establishments with dubious credentials, charge between £35 and £50 per week.

Four advertisements in the local daily newspaper and a leafleting campaign during September and October resulted in a flood of enquiries from executive parents and their employers. A week of commercials on the local radio station in November produced another inundation. Finally, an Open Day, also in November, covered editorially by the local evening paper, attracted a large number of parents and several requests for placements. The catchment area proved to be much wider than the city itself, and prospective customers included single mothers, job sharers and part-timers as well as full-time executives and professionals. The total cost of promotion in preparing for the opening was less than £4,000.

However, despite strengths in product, place and people, the number of children actually registered to start in January is insufficient to fulfil the forecasts made in the business plan. Disappointed by her failure to attract sufficient customers despite favourable pre-opening indications, Mrs Ash has asked a friend who has recently taken a marketing diploma course to prepare a new marketing communications programme for 1996.

Question

You are to act the role of the friend and are required to produce a marketing communications plan in report form. This should include budget recommendations. Use language that Mrs Ash will readily understand. You may make reasonable assumptions about information not given in the case. These assumptions should be briefly stated and justified.   **(50 marks)**

*   *   *   *   *

DIPLOMA IN MARKETING
MARKETING COMMUNICATIONS STRATEGY

Time: $1\frac{1}{2}$ hours
Total: 50 marks

Case 9.3: The Big Cat's on the prowl

You are asked to play the role of marketing communications manager for Jaguar.

Jaguar is a British-based, luxury car manufacturer which markets its product on a worldwide basis. The company is now owned by Ford, which bought Jaguar in 1990 for £1.6 billion, partly reflecting the value of the brand. Worldwide sales reached 50000 cars in 1988, but then followed a period of recession which has badly affected luxury car sales. By 1992 sales had fallen to less than 25000. The new owners, Ford, however, were much more optimistic and are now planning for worldwide sales of 100000 by the end of the century. This represents a massive challenge for marketing and marketing communications.

Jaguar is already active in most developed countries, but is planning a massive push over the next five years into new markets – South America, Asia, Eastern Europe and Russia in particular. Over this period £700 million will be invested in new product development. The marketing director of Jaguar states: 'Our task over the rest of this decade is to make Jaguar more like the company it was in 1960, with a wider model range.' The speed and scale of the changes ahead represent a severe challenge for Jaguar. 'It's going to be a very interesting balance between bringing in all the new technology and maintaining Jaguar's much prized reputation as a brand which holds its price well in the second-hand market,' says the marketing director.

1994 proved a better year for Jaguar, with bullish signs in the four key markets of Germany, the USA, Japan and the UK. The pick-up was in part due to the devaluation of the pound but radical changes in product and marketing strategy also played their part. The new models came with an unprecedented range of technological upgrades, most visibly the driver's side airbag and a new alarm system, both as standard. To tempt buyers there was a three-year/60000-miles warranty which had catapulted Jaguar ahead of many of its luxury rivals in Europe.

Another sign of the new marketing revolution taking hold at Jaguar was its bold new buy-back initiative. If purchasers were unhappy with their car, they had 30 days in which to return it and receive a full refund.

The move proved incredibly successful, with less than 2 per cent returned and half of these exchanged for another model. This programme has helped Jaguar increase its rating in customer satisfaction surveys in the USA.

Jaguar management realize that substantial investment will be necessary in their marketing communication strategy if they are to achieve their ambitious marketing objectives. They have appointed the international advertising agency, J. Walter Thompson, to handle their account. The campaigns being planned will once again focus on the enormous emotional appeal of the brand. The company wants its public to say: Jaguar is back in a big way, in a highly visible way.'

The company has asked its agency to explore every element of the marketing communications mix. In the UK, the company's bread and butter market, £3 million has been earmarked for an advertising campaign and, equally important, the below-the-line activity has been boosted with a budget of £750 000. The company has also revealed that it wants a better use of its 36 000-customer database. The marketing director believes that, with the decline in the number of luxury car customers, 'it is not difficult actually to communicate with every one of them, so long as you're very careful about how you select your promotions and your direct mail. Once you've got them, you make sure that you give them what they want.'

In the past, car manufacturers may have been guilty of last-minute marketing, believing that a great product, supported by a lot of expensive advertising, would be greedily snapped up by an admiring and grateful public. It is now realized that this will not do in the new area of lifestyle targeting. The average age of the Jaguar customer is 50 years old, and the company wants to bring that down. The company's plans include a much more accessible model, codenamed X200, scheduled for production by 1998. Currently the XJ6 model costs less than £35 000 and has recently been voted 'best luxury car' against competition from the more expensive Lexus, BMW 740i and Mercedes 600 SEL. A sports car version of the XJ6 is to be launched, which will attract younger customers. At the top end of the range is the Jaguar XJ12 and the Daimler Double Six, costing over £50 000. These are more clearly differentiated than in the past, with the Jaguar being aimed at the 'driving enthusiast' and the Daimler, with a more elegant and restrained ride, for the ranks of company chairmen, who remain key to the car's success.

(*Source*: Interview given by Jaguar's marketing director to *Marketing* magazine).

Question

In your capacity as the marketing communications manager of Jaguar, you have been asked to prepare notes to be discussed at an important meeting with your advertising agency, to assist them fully in planning the effective promotion of the Jaguar brand on an international basis over the next five years. These notes should be structured to provide clear guidelines for the agency on positioning, media selection, creative rationale, budgeting and monitoring. **(50 marks)**

★　★　★　★　★

DIPLOMA IN MARKETING
MARKETING COMMUNICATIONS STRATEGY

Time: $1\frac{1}{2}$ **hours**
Total: 50 marks

Case 9.4: Dennison Aggregates

The market research findings were clear enough. The question troubling Donald Black, marketing manager of Dennison Aggregates Ltd, was how best to use them.

A new product, codenamed RRM, had emerged from the research and development programme of Dennison's parent company, one of Britain's major quarrying groups. It was a 'bagged ready-to-use retarded mortar' for large-scale brickwork applications.

The parent group had pioneered ready-mixed mortar in 1978. They would now be the first to offer on-site delivery in specially designed 50-kg containers which can be forklifted or crane-slung to the point of use as and when required.

The fact that RRM is factory mixed before delivery eliminates the doubt about quality control that is inevitable when the operation is performed by a labourer with a shovel, bags of cement, a pile of sand and a cement mixer. The containers can be delivered to any site within 24 hours. 'Retardation' allows the mortar to remain workable for about 36 hours thereafter.

The dimensions of the containers, holding 0.3 cubic metres, make it possible to move mortar in bulk to high-level or cramped sites at which labourers would otherwise have to move manageable volumes by wheelbarrow at frequent intervals.

The market research report on Donald Black's desk contained the results of telephone interviews with a representative sample of builders' merchants and building contractors in two major cities. It showed, among many other findings, that builders' merchants generally had a negative attitude to both the idea and the product. They foresaw ordering difficulties because of the short shelf life and tended to dismiss the product as being only for very small contractors and the do-it-yourself market. The research report suggested that 'it seems clear that they will wait for demand to materialize rather than take the initiative and carry stock'.

Building contractors, on the other hand, responded enthusiastically to the product characteristics. They especially welcomed the prospect of a consistent mix, good workability, pre-mix convenience and labour-saving efficiency. The report remarked on the attitude-scaling scores as being 'among the highest and most uniform encountered among commercial surveys carried out since 1983'.

Builders' merchants anticipated a price of £2.00 per bag, while building contractors expected to pay about £3.00.

Headquarters had decided to go to market. Donald Black now had to set up a briefing meeting with Dennison's advertising agency, specialists in business-to-business advertising, who would need to plan a campaign which could convert latent demand into actual sales.

The budget would ultimately be decided by the parent company, but Dennison's total sales in the previous year had been £40 million.

Question

Prepare a formal document to be tabled at Donald Black's meeting with the agency, using the information available to you and structured appropriately for the stated purpose. **(50 marks)**

★　★　★　★　★

DIPLOMA IN MARKETING
INTERNATIONAL MARKETING STRATEGY

Time: $1\frac{1}{2}$ hours
Total: 50 marks

Case 9.5: Star Engineering

The annual planning process was well under way at the London headquarters of Star Engineering. In two weeks' time the final international marketing plan must be presented to the board of directors.

Star Engineering was established in 1910. It had grown from a local to a regional and then a national company. In the 1970s the company became active in exporting. It had been particularly successful in the Middle East and in South East Asia. Competition was particularly strong in the United States and in Germany. Because of this, Star had, in the past, made a policy decision to avoid entering these two markets. Star currently has 65 per cent of the UK market, in total worth £20 million. In the Middle East it has 20 per cent of a market worth approximately £10 million, while in South East Asia it has 25 per cent of a market worth £18 million.

The main strategic thrust of the planning process this year is an expressed corporate aim to move towards world leadership, or, as the company chairman preferred to call it, to become the world Star, instead of a rather modest world player.

Company sales turnover for 1995 had grown by only 1 per cent, to £21 million. The world recession impacted particularly severely on the civil engineering industry, Star's main customer group, so in all the circumstances a 1 per cent increase was a very creditable performance. Net profits, on the other hand, were reduced by 11 per cent, to £1.6 million.

During the 1980s Star Engineering began a process of becoming a more international company. Initially all non-UK sales came from exporting. However, sales offices were set up in Kuwait and in Singapore. Later, a distribution depot was established in Singapore. This helped sales through improved customer services and the reassurance to customers created by Star's tangible presence.

In the future the company intends to manufacture in several other sites in addition to the UK. This would create some benefits for Star's international performance, but would also involve increased risks, particularly those created by political change.

The company needs to develop a more international marketing culture. Currently, it is unsure how to proceed.

Question

(a) Evaluate the organizational control and marketing implications of moving from a modest international marketing approach to the approach required to achieve the corporate aim of world leadership.   **(25 marks)**

(b) What approach would you propose to Star Engineering for evaluating existing and new overseas markets given its existing level of expertise and involvement?   **(25 marks)**

★   ★   ★   ★   ★

DIPLOMA IN MARKETING
INTERNATIONAL MARKETING STRATEGY

Time: $1\frac{1}{2}$ hours
Total: 50 marks

Case 9.6: Leisureworld Bicycles

Leisureworld is a company which specializes in marketing consumer goods products through appropriate retail and other distribution channels. Eighty-eight per cent of sales are to Western European countries, with 10 per cent to the USA and 2 per cent to Canada. The company is not a manufacturer: it buys (or sources) its products from around the world. If assembly is required, as it is for bicycles, this is arranged with an appropriate manufacturer. The finished bicycle is always branded with the Leisureworld name.

The strong upsurge in demand in the bicycle market during the 1980s and the early 1990s was an attraction for Leisureworld. With the company mission centred on leisure, bicycles provide a clear and close fit in many country markets.

The bicycle market is influenced by fashion and fitness trends, the weather, the quality and safeness of the road and other cycle track infrastructure, and by the lack of hills. Regions in flat areas – for example, the Northern Italian plain, The Netherlands, and Beijing in China – all have very large cycle-owning and using populations.

Over the past fifteen years different forms of bicycle have become popular. In the early 1980s adult small-wheel bikes were in vogue; later, children's all-purpose tough BMX were introduced and achieved substantial sales in most advanced industrial countries. Mountain bikes, introduced via California in the late 1980s, made a dramatic impact.

Bicycles are aimed at many different market segments. In the more affluent markets in the world, leisure, fitness and cycle racing take the majority of the market. In addition, bicycles specifically made for children are an important part of sales, accounting for up to half of the total market by volume in most industrially advanced countries. While there is a market for bicycles as a means of basic transport in all countries, it is in the lesser developed and the developing countries around the world that this segment is highly significant.

Mike Bowen, international marketing manager of Leisureworld, is currently trying to resolve a particular problem. In 1995 bicycles accounted for 27 per cent of Leisureworld's £146 million turnover. Unfortunately, the impact of the recession in many markets, and the considerable penetration achieved in many country markets for mountain bikes, resulted in a saturated and overstocked market during 1994 and 1995.

A new craze in bicycles might start at any time. However, at the moment there is no evidence of what form that might take. Product modification and price cutting are the main approaches being taken at present.

Production of bicycles in low-cost countries – for example, China and Taiwan – is a threat to the established manufacturers such as Raleigh in the UK and Peugeot in France. Leisureworld, by sourcing from whatever they regard as the best source at the time, is able to keep its costs low. Another important factor in this market is the substantial success of Shimano, a Japanese manufacturer of a wide range of component parts such as gears and pedals. Shimano is a highly innovative company and has succeeded in creating a high demand for its parts. In effect, it is now difficult to sell bicycles in many markets without Shimano components. The points of difference between many bicycles are often related to company and brand name, colour and graphics, distribution outlet and price.

To add to Mike Bowen's workload, Leisureworld has been offered a share in a top cycle racing team. The team will compete in the major road-racing events around the world, including the high-prestige, month-long Tour de France. If Leisureworld accepts this opportunity, the major part of its bicycle marketing communications budget of £0.9 million would be devoted to the costs of the cycle team and the related publicity surrounding each cycle race.

Question

As an adviser on international marketing retained by Leisureworld:

(a) Propose and justify the ways in which the company should carry out market segmentation on the world bicycle market. **(30 marks)**
(b) Examine the advantages and disadvantages of using most of the bicycle marketing communications budget on the cycle racing team. On the assumption that Leisureworld goes ahead with the cycle racing team, explain how the racing team could be used by Leisureworld Bicycles in its international marketing communications. **(20 marks)**

★　★　★　★　★

DIPLOMA IN MARKETING
INTERNATIONAL MARKETING STRATEGY

Time: $1\frac{1}{2}$ hours
Total: 50 marks

Case 9.7: Teesside Electrical

Discussions for the first marketing research fact-finding trip were still not finalized over a tea and biscuits meeting at the north-east England headquarters of Teesside Electrical. The trip, planned over the past two months by Bill Murphy, export manager of Teesside Electrical, still needed more work.

The company, one of several owned by a major UK conglomerate, was anxious to expand the export earnings of the company. The company had a range of electrical products, but specialized in lightning protection. Electrical storm damage can be prevented by the use of appropriate copper or aluminium rods fixed onto the sides of buildings to allow the safe passage of the lightning charge from the top of the building to the ground. It is possible to coat the copper or aluminium rods to give a more pleasing appearance or to integrate them into the design of the building. The company's markets were to major building contractors, as a small but important part of the building process. A range of people were connected with this process, from architects, the main contractor, to subcontractors and sometimes down to installers, often steeplejacks.

Teesside Electrical is well-established in the UK. Until recently, it relied heavily on the UK and Middle East markets, of which Kuwait and Iraq were, until the invasion of Kuwait in 1990, very important players. Eighty-one per cent of sales in 1989 were to the UK, 19 per cent were exported. Two-thirds of exports went to Kuwait and Iraq. The remaining 6 per cent, a turnover of £2.7 million, were sold to other countries in the Middle East, Malaysia, Singapore, Hong Kong and Australia.

The marked recession in the UK, worse than any that the executives at Teesside could recall, plus the earlier loss of almost £5.5 million in the Middle East, had made life difficult. To make matters worse, the expected up-turn in Kuwaiti business had been slow to materialize.

Perhaps belatedly, the company was looking to Europe to replace lost sales. Teesside had picked up sporadic orders from Swedish, German, French and Italian building contractors, usually for building contracts in the Middle East or in South East Asia. What was of some concern was the development of harmonized EC standards for electrical and lightning protection products. If the standards were more favourable to manufacturers in other EC countries, Teesside would have to invest in new tools to manufacture to the new standard.

Teesside Electrical had a strong sales force of ten people. Because of the nature of its business it did not rely on agents. In important markets, the company established a resident salesperson. In other markets, it relied on a planned sales visit programme. A half-yearly cycle of visits was made to the country concerned to identify suitable building projects and to influence the decision-making process concerning the quality of the products and services provided by Teesside. Once a potential project was identified, visits were made as necessary in order to secure the contract.

Some of the parts manufactured by Teesside were not particularly complicated, but the range of specialized experts on lightning protection was a key factor in success. Electrical storms could cause significant damage to unprotected or badly protected buildings, and the long-term evaluation of lightning damage and different types of lightning protection systems and methods of installation gave Teesside a competitive edge over less sophisticated manufacturers.

The decision to look at Europe had been taken rather reluctantly because Teesside was aware of the considerable adjustment that might be required in order to be successful with European customers. No-one in the company was particularly proficient in any other European language – a recent languages audit of the staff showed a few employees with a limited social conversation competence in French and others in German. No other European languages were spoken, with the exception of some Danish (the sea link between north-east England and Denmark meant that shopping trips and cultural exchange programmes had created an interest in Denmark).

Until now all the promotional literature and technical data sheets had been produced in English but only rarely in other languages. The company visited trade fairs from time to time, but had never taken an exhibition stand.

The fact-finding trip had taken several months to plan because of the difficulty of knowing which approach to take and which countries to visit. Bill Murphy was anxious that the trip should yield high-quality information which could be acted upon quickly. With the weak sales figures, both domestic and export, a fast reliable response was essential.

Question

(*a*) As an international marketing consultant, you have been asked to advise Bill Murphy on the choice of country, or countries, that he should visit on his fact-finding mission. Justify your choice(s) and indicate the factors that you feel are appropriate in making such a choice. (**25 marks**)

(*b*) On the assumption that:
   (i) marketing research evidence shows worthwhile opportunities for Teesside in Europe;
   (ii) Teesside can only afford to exhibit at one trade fair in Europe over the next twelve months;
   what general factors would you take into account in deciding which trade fair to select? (**5 marks**)

(*c*) Examine how other elements in the promotional mix should be used by Teesside as part of its expansion into Europe. (**20 marks**)

* * * * *

DIPLOMA IN MARKETING
INTERNATIONAL MARKETING STRATEGY

Time: $1\frac{1}{2}$ hours
Total: 50 marks

Case 9.8: Giant's Castle Games Ltd

The company was formed at the beginning of the 1980s to take advantage of the exciting developments in computer games. Andrew Marsden was and is the marketing entrepreneur for Giant's Castle; Chris Culley is the creative genius on the software side.

The 1980s were a time of rapid development. Andrew Marsden worked for over ten years in the USA and Canada with companies marketing fast-moving consumer goods. Family reasons caused him to return to the UK. His return coincided with the boom in home computers, created in the UK by Clive Sinclair. A whole series of small cottage-industry-type companies were set up to exploit a new market in computer games. These games required graphics and software programming. Later on, sound also became an ingredient of successful games.

Chris Culley was drawn into the industry because of her fascination with computer games, and was soon developing successful games which were sold by mail order. She was introduced to Andrew Marsden in 1982. Shortly after this, Giant's Castle Games Ltd was formed. The first three years of trading were very successful. The chief difficulty lay in creating the 'right' games. The main marketing tasks were to gain favourable press reviews in the myriad of computer magazines and to place mail order advertisements.

The mid-1980s saw changes in the computer games market. The quick, easy profits, often highly publicized in the tabloids, resulted in many new entrants to the market, and it became more difficult to develop the 'right' games.

The original computer games market was built around the Sinclair Spectrum and other home computers, for example, Atari and Commodore. A later development was the specialized games console from companies such as the Japanese Nintendo and Sega. These companies were already experienced in arcade games machines, and now produced smaller home-based games consoles at prices comparable with home computers.

Games console manufacturers did not, however, have the expertise to develop games, and without exciting games the console attached to the TV set was not very attractive. A key difficulty for Giant's Castle was the change in distribution channel. The market was not only becoming more international, but the mail-order approach no longer worked for the games console software suppliers.

To be successful, Giant's Castle needed to excite the games console companies. The game would then be placed on a list of accepted games. The company then had to persuade distribution companies called 'publishers' to buy their accepted games. Publishers are, in fact, very much like distributors in that they buy the product, distribute and promote it within a certain area.

Andrew and Chris decided to review the situation at a beer and sandwiches meeting at their South London offices. They summarized their meeting on the office flipchart with the following bullet points:

Problems

- Creating suitable games for Nintendo and other console systems.
- Financing equipment costs.
- Financing software development.
- Retaining key staff.
- Persuading more publishers to take and sell Giant's Castle games.
- The need to become a more international marketing company.

Andrew carried out some low-cost marketing research in the UK and the USA through personal visits and through conversations with publishers. A major comment was the bad press on the large amount of time spent by young people playing computer console games. Was there an opportunity for more interesting and involving software programs? Currently about 50 per cent of all games consoles were sold in the USA, 30 per cent in Japan and most of the rest were sold in Europe. Europe was thought to be a growth market, but some other markets were also important (for example, Canada).

Chris Culley was becoming increasingly concerned about the difficulty in finding the 'right' games. She had ten teams of three people each working on the programmes for different games and approaches. Each team consisted of a computer programmer, a graphics designer and a sound person. It takes about one year to work from the concept to the finalization of a game. A few were winners; most were not.

The company relied on Andrew to sell the products to publishers. Until now almost all Giant's Castle games had been sold in the UK. The importance of the non-UK market was becoming more and more apparent, but Andrew was not sure how the games would 'travel'.

To be successful, to survive in the future, the company needs to make some substantial changes. It also needs to implement some quick deals to improve cash flow. Of the nine accepted games, only one had been really successful. Unfortunately, the successful phase has now passed. Christmas 1995 is only two weeks away, and the Christmas 1996 trade fairs in the US and European markets will take place in early spring 1996.

Question

(*a*) Examine the main strategic decisions in international marketing that Giant's Castle needs to take over the next five years. **(25 marks)**

(*b*) Identify one of the above decisions in international markets facing Giant's Castle. Develop a structured approach to show how this should be implemented. **(25 marks)**

★ ★ ★ ★ ★

Time: $1\frac{1}{2}$ hours
Total: 50 marks

Case 9.9: Anderson Marine Construction Ltd

Anderson Marine Construction (AMC) is a well-established and financially successful builder of medium-sized, high-performance yachts and power-boats. Based on the south coast of England, the company's products have developed a strong reputation for quality and performance, and an intensely loyal and knowledgeable customer base.

The company has traditionally adopted a largely reactive approach to selling, justifying this partly on the grounds that for the past twenty years it has been able to sell everything it has been able to make, and partly because the firm's founder and managing director, Tom Anderson, saw the firm facing little direct competition in its principal target markets. After the early 1990s, however, sales began to drop as demand for expensive luxury goods declined. As a response to this, AMC cut its prices by 6 per cent in real terms for the 1994 season and then by a further 4 per cent for 1995. Despite this, sales remained sluggish.

Faced with this situation, and with no sight of an upturn in demand, Tom Anderson called in a marketing consultant to advise on what AMC should do next. The consultant argued that further price cuts were likely to achieve little and that in the long term they would probably be detrimental to the image developed by AMC. Instead, he suggested that AMC should capitalize upon its reputation and the very strong brand values associated with its name by moving down the size and price scale by developing a new range of smaller and lower priced boats. Although this sector of the market had a greater number of direct competitors, the consultant suggested that patterns of demand would be more consistent and less susceptible to fluctuations in the economy.

Although the idea had an initial appeal, Anderson recognized that the company's approach to marketing and selling would have to change. Previously, the firm's sales effort had been limited to very occasional advertisements in the boating press and a small stand every other year at a regional boat show. This, together with the strength of the company's reputation and word of mouth recommendation had, he felt, been adequate. Boats were made to order with a delivery time of nine to fifteen months, and prices, which were negotiated individually with clients, reflected the specification demanded. Once completed, they were either delivered by AMC or customers collected the boats themselves.

The consultant emphasized that the new range would need to be targeted at buyers whose sailing skills and buying motives and processes were very different from those of AMC's traditional customers. The implications of this were spelled out in a report:

1 Buyers within the proposed target group would be less knowledgeable about boats and sailing and would expect a greater degree of what he referred to as 'active selling' of the product's benefits.
2 There would be a need for a structured distribution network with at least ten distributors throughout the country.
3 Buyers would not be prepared to wait for delivery but would expect boats to be available from stock.
4 A communications programme would be required.
5 A formal pricing and distributor discount structure would be needed.
6 Because the new range would bring AMC into more direct competition with other boat builders, a competitive monitoring system should be developed.
7 A marketing budget should be set as a matter of priority and the responsibilities for the marketing effort clearly allocated.

Question

Recognizing that these recommendations called for a far more proactive approach to marketing than had previously been adopted, Anderson decided to appoint a marketing manager. As the person appointed to this post, you have the immediate responsibility for developing the marketing plan to support the new range, which is scheduled for launch for the 1996 sailing season. You are therefore required to:

(a) Prepare an outline of the marketing plan for the launch and subsequent market development of the new range. In doing this, you should make specific reference to the nature of any additional information that you might require. **(35 marks)**
(b) In the light of AMC's previous approaches to selling, what, if any, organizational problems might you expect to encounter in implementing the marketing plan? In what ways might these problems be overcome or minimized? **(15 marks)**

* * * * *

DIPLOMA IN MARKETING
PLANNING AND CONTROL

Time: $1\frac{1}{2}$ hours
Total: 50 marks

Case 9.10: *Watergate Pumps Ltd*

Watergate Pumps Ltd manufactures and markets a range of water pumps and control systems for domestic and industrial central heating systems. For the past three years total industry sales of domestic pumps have been stable, at an average of 1.3 million units per annum (£40 million at manufacturers' average selling prices). Sales are forecast to increase only slowly over the next few years and are expected to reach a peak of 1.55 million units per annum in 1999

Within the domestic sector, there are four principal markets for the product: local authorities, the public utilities such as British Gas, regional/national building companies, and small firms of builders/plumbers and individuals repairing their own heating systems.

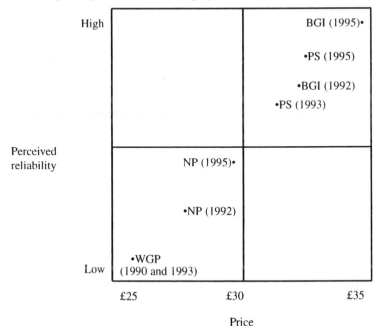

Figure 1(a)   Competitive positioning (1992 and 1995)

Table 1 Selected market data

	Market shares within the domestic pumps sector (1992–1995)				Total manufacturing capacity (000 units)	Total output in 1995 (000 units)	UK/ overseas split of sales in 1995
	1992 (%)	1993 (%)	1994 (%)	1995 (%)			
Watergate Pumps	35	29	27	24	475	320	100/0
BG Industrial	50	50	48	48	850	830	75/25
Northern Pumps	15	13	15	16	300	280	74/26
Pump Suppliers	0	8	10	12	300	300	52/48

Source: Trade figures.

Table 2 Market and competitor data

	Sales in 1995 by type of buyer (000 units)	Expected percentage increase/ (decrease) by 1999	Market position of each company by type of buyer (1995)			
			No. 1	No. 2	No. 3	No. 4
Local authorities	400	(25)	WGP	NP	PS	BGI
Public utilities	300	66	BGI	PS	WGP	NP
Regional/national builders	400	25	BGI	PS	NP	WGP
Local builders/plumbers and private individuals	200	25	BGI	NP	PS	WGP

Key: WGP – Watergate Pumps
BGI – BG Industrial
NP – Northern Pumps
PS – Pump Suppliers

Source: Trade data.

Table 3 Rank order of the principal buying motives of different customer groups

	Local authorities	Public utilities	Regional/ national builders	Local builders/ plumbers and private individuals
Price	1	3	3 =	3
Availability off the shelf	N/A	N/A	3 =	1 =
Reliability	3	1	1	4
Ease of fitting	2	2	2	1 =

N/A: Not applicable, since supplies are delivered in bulk to regional warehouse.

Source: Compiled from trade data.

The company, which is a subsidiary of a far larger organization which has interests throughout the building supplies industry, has three competitors. Selected market data collected from various sources appear in Tables 1, 2 and 3.

Watergate has been taken by surprise by a variety of developments in the marketplace over the past few years, including:

High

NP (1995)•	BGI (1995)•
	BGI (1992)•
•WGP (1992)	PS (1995)•
	PS (1993)•
NP (1992)•	
•WGP (1995)	

Availability

Low

Low   High

Perceived ease of fitting

Key: WGP – Watergate Pumps
    BGI – BG Industrial
    NP – Northern Pumps
    PS – Pump Suppliers
Source: Internal planning document.

Figure 1(b)

- the entry to the market in 1993 of Pump Suppliers, a Dutch-owned company which set up a factory in southern England
- the launch by BG Industrial (BGI) and Northern Pumps of several modified and new products
- a general competitive repositioning (see Figure 1)
- an extension by all three competitors of the guarantees offered on their products from one to three years
- the three-year stagnation of the market
- a significant shift in customers' buying motives, with quality and ease of fitting having become increasingly important
- a series of improvements by all three competitors in their control systems
- the move by BGI and Northern Pumps into a number of profitable overseas markets.

Because of this, there is now recognition that the company's understanding of the market is poor and that some form of structured external environment monitoring is needed.

Question

(a) As the company's newly appointed market analyst, you are required to prepare a detailed report for the marketing director, recommending how an effective external environmental monitoring system for the company might best be developed and implemented. Included within the report should be your suggestions on the structure of the system, the expected inputs and outputs, the probable organizational and resource implications and the nature of any benefits that should emerge. **(30 marks)**

(b) In the light of the information contained in the mini-case, what recommendations for future marketing action would you make? **(20 marks)**

★   ★   ★   ★   ★

DIPLOMA IN MARKETING
PLANNING AND CONTROL

Time: $1\frac{1}{2}$ hours
Total: 50 marks

Case 9.11 : Penton Ltd

Penton is a medium-sized company which manufactures and markets a range of DIY products under the Easi-way brand name. Its performance over the past ten years, a period during which the market for DIY products has grown rapidly, has been viewed by those within the industry as steady but generally unimpressive. In particular, its critics have pointed to performance levels that are below the industry norm, a reliance upon its long-established and now old-fashioned distribution networks, low levels of advertising spend, a failure to exploit the potential strength of the brand name and a poor profit performance.

Towards the end of 1994, the company was the subject of a takeover bid from a smaller but more aggressive and far more successful competitor. Although Penton's board managed to fight off the bid, the sudden awareness of the company's vulnerability to further bids has led to a reassessment of its entire manufacturing and marketing strategy.

The problems being faced by the company were exacerbated by the downturn in retail sales which began to affect the economy at the end of the 1980s. Faced with what was proving to be a static sales curve and a reducing profit margin, the decision was taken to bring in a firm of marketing consultants to conduct a detailed audit of the company and make recommendations for future strategy. The consultants' initial report highlighted a number of areas of concern which, they suggested, should be the focus of attention.

1 The company's strong production orientation and a lack of marketing representation at board level.
2 A largely reactive managerial philosophy.
3 Little long-term product or market planning.
4 An over-reliance upon a small number of ageing products.
5 A poorly structured new product planning process.
6 The generally disappointing performance and high failure rate of new product launches over the past few years.
7 A failure to exploit the potential strength of the brand name.
8 Increasing pressures upon margins.

The environmental analysis proved to be more encouraging, with the consultants giving prominence to the size and long-term growth potential of the DIY market and the major profit opportunities offered by new products.

They also pointed to the high level of retail concentration in the market, the need for organizations in this sector to be proactive in their new product development and for new products to be supported by a strong promotional campaign.

The evaluation of the company's manufacturing capabilities suggested that there is a need for investment in new plant. With regard to the research and development area, the conclusion was that 'while' the area has potential and the R and D staff are enthusiastic and highly qualified, the activity has suffered from a lack of direction. As a result, the majority of new products have not been related sufficiently directly to market demands.'

Against the background of these findings, the board has attempted to identify the areas of greatest priority and has decided to focus upon the three areas which it believes require the most immediate attention. These are the development of:

- a marketing orientation
- a far stronger and more effective planning culture
- a structured and productive new product development process.

Question
(a) As a member of the team of consultants, you have the responsibility for making recommendations as to how the company might most effectively achieve this. You are therefore required to prepare a report showing how this might be done. **(30 marks)**
(b) What are the implications of your suggestions for approaches to management control? **(20 marks)**

★   ★   ★   ★   ★

DIPLOMA IN MARKETING
PLANNING AND CONTROL

Time: $1\frac{1}{2}$ hours
Total: 50 marks

Case 9.12: New Directions plc

New Directions is a high street fashion chain which was founded in the late 1950s. After twenty years of slow and generally unspectacular growth, a new managing director, Thomas Oakley, was appointed in 1981. Under his very different and aggressively entrepreneurial management style, the company underwent a decade of explosive growth. Many of the old staff left during this period and a far younger team was recruited. The new staff were given considerable operating freedom and high salaries, but were expected to achieve performance levels well above the industry average. By 1988, the company had 400 stores and had become one of the major players in the young (15–25), C1/C2 male and female fashion sectors. Its reputation in the City was that of an ambitious, design-oriented company led by an unconventional, abrasive and maverick figure who inspired considerable loyalty among his employees.

At the beginning of 1990 the company was bought out by a large and cash-rich conglomerate whose financial performance over the preceding decade had proved to be consistently strong. Despite this, the group's senior management was viewed by the City as being generally staid and unimaginative. The group overall was viewed as having a strong financial orientation with an emphasis upon systems and control. Strategy at the group level was perceived as being risk-aversive.

New Directions' managing director and small senior management team quickly found that operating within a group in which they were accountable to the group's main board constrained their entrepreneurial style and traditional freedom. Not only were they faced with the need to make out a strong written case for anything other than a minor change in strategy but, as they saw it, major restrictions were placed on their ability to capitalize upon short-term opportunities. Profits were remitted to the centre, and each division's managing director was then required to bid for sums for capital expenditure on an annual basis.

After two years in succession in which his plans for development were rejected by the main board, Oakley resigned. At the heart of the disagreement was his belief that New Directions needed to move up the quality scale and both up and down the age scale. The demographic changes taking place would, he argued, lead to a cut of at least 20 per cent in the size of the company's traditional target market over the next few years. The company should therefore chase the demographic shift by targeting the 30–40-year-olds, a sector in which annual growth of 12 per cent was being forecast. At the same time, he suggested, a new chain should be developed which would appeal to the children's market. 'Children', he said, 'are the ultimate fashion accessory. We need to capitalize on this.'

He also pointed to the research evidence which suggested that buyers wanted better quality, something for which New Directions had never had a particularly strong reputation. Instead, the company had concentrated on developing a strong fashion element at 'popular' prices. While this strategy had undoubtedly been successful, there was now a need to begin the process of making a series of fundamental changes. Oakley also argued for the need for a rethink in the approach to store design. Competition from other retail chains had become ever more aggressive during the early 1990s, and evidence existed to suggest that buyers were looking for new and more exciting shopping experiences. An essential element in this was the retail concept, something which had taken a significant step forward in the early 1990s in the repositioning and renaming of one of the company's major competitors. Oakley also pointed to the need to begin looking towards opportunities overseas. 'The British market', he suggested, 'offers only limited scope for growth. We need to get into some of the other European markets and particularly Spain.' He went on to point out that the Spanish market was growing at a faster rate than any other. Indeed, without telling the main board or getting its agreement, he had already gone ahead with plans to begin selling into one of the largest chains of Spanish fashion stores.

Each of these arguments was rejected by the main board on the grounds of cost and perceived risk.

Following Oakley's resignation, the group appointed as his replacement one of their fast-track corporate finance staff. With little direct retailing experience, he set about reorganizing the company. In doing this, he slashed Oakley's plans for development. Largely because of this, a significant number of the team who had worked with Oakley and who very largely saw themselves as his protégés left. In most cases they were snapped up by competitors who placed considerable value on the training and experience to which they had been exposed.

As the recession of the mid-1990s continued to bite, turnover dropped. The new managing director's almost desperate response was to pursue an aggressive price-cutting policy and to reduce overheads as far as possible.

The annual strategic review at the end of 1994 (two years after Oakley's replacement had taken over) painted a dismal picture. Sales were down, market share was slipping, staff were demoralized and, as a market research report highlighted, the image of the chain in the 15–25, 25–30 and 30–40 age groups was confused. In short, New Directions was no longer a leader or even a serious player in the young fashion market.

Question

(a) Prepare a SWOT analysis of the company both for the period before the takeover and for the period reached at the end of the case study. Having done this, discuss the implications of *One* of your analyses for methods of marketing planning and control.   **(30 marks)**

(*b*) As a consultant to the company and in the light of the findings of the strategic review, what course(s) of action would you recommend should be taken?   **(20 marks)**

★ ★ ★ ★ ★

10 *Certificate level: mini-case specimen answers*

Case 8.1: Fine Furnishings Limited

Answer

Report: Marketing at Fine Furnishings Limited
To: Main Board
From: A Marketing Consultant

1 Introduction

This report advises Fine Furnishings Limited with regard to the following:

(a) Product mix (including company image)
(b) Stockholding policy and customer service
(c) Suggested promotional activities.

2 Product mix

There is no doubt that the current company policy with regard to the product mix is costly to support.

As you know, Fine Furnishings Limited currently offers one of the most complete and varied product mixes on the market. Not only is the product mix 'wide' – being composed of a complete range of product lines for furnishing the office, e.g. carpets, desks, chairs, safes, etc. – but within each line there is also considerable 'depth', with a great many variations of each product being offered. For example, you currently offer some 42 different designs of chairs and 23 varieties of office desks.

Combined with your stockholding policy (see Part 3 of this report), and the current downturn in trade due to the recession, your product mix policy is causing severe liquidity and profitability problems.

Another important facet of your product mix is the emphasis on quality and superior design/technical specifications. This, too, because of the recession, is causing you problems. As you are well aware, competition is now intense in all markets. We know that increasingly specified purchases of office furniture are stressing price as the key factor in supplier choice. The emphasis at Fine Furnishings, of course, has always been value for money.

Given these problems, it might be tempting to suggest that the solutions should be based on offering a more restricted product range together with a more basic specification and hence lower prices for the products. Alternatively, at the very least, perhaps one might be tempted to introduce a 'budget' range. However, although tempting, it is strongly recommended that none of these directions of change to the product mix should be adopted. The reasons are as follows.

Company image

At the moment the company is known for its quality products which are sturdily constructed and its extremely comprehensive product range which enables the matching of design and colour. The company's reputation in this respect has been built up over many years. Any attempt to move 'downmarket' with a more restricted product range, or even the introduction of a budget range, would, in our view, detract from the quality image of the company.

Strengths and weaknesses

The strengths of the company lie with its ability to keep in touch with advances in the office furniture field and offer good design, workmanship, value for money and technical specifications. However, the company is simply not geared up to a cost leadership strategy.

Even if Fine Furnishings was tempted to reduce price temporarily, you would find it very difficult to return to the necessarily higher prices which your quality products require.

Our major suggestion with regard to the product mix, therefore, is to retain the emphasis on quality and variety while at the same time implementing an effective stock control and production planning system in order to minimize inventories (see Part 3 of this report). At the same time there needs to be a much stronger emphasis on the value-for-money elements of the product mix which in turn need effective and focused promotion (see Part 4 of this report).

3 Stockholding policy and customer service

As mentioned earlier, the temptation would be to cut back significantly on all stock, extending delivery dates and reducing the range of spares which are currently offered. However, as suggested in Part 2 of the report, your current stockholding policy and approach to customer service represent the unique sales propositions (USPs) of your business. The suggestion, therefore, is to keep the same levels of stock and the same stockholding policy but to have improved systems of stock control and production planning.

One suggestion is that manufacturers keep stocks for immediate delivery, with Fine Furnishings Limited selling from catalogues or stocking and not paying for the goods until they are sold. Obviously this would release working capital and is worth exploring with manufacturers. This is not as curious as it might seem, as, for example, many car dealers now have arrangements with their manufacturers similar to this. Manufacturers might go along with the suggestion rather than lose the business.

Careful attention should be paid to stock control and planning systems so as to maintain current levels of customer service at minimum cost.

4 Suggestions for promotional activity

Overall levels of promotional activity must be increased. This might seem difficult given current levels of sales and profitability, but in the long term increased budget for promotion will pay off. As important as increasing promotional budgets is the focus of promotional activity and particularly the message which should be emphasized. The following themes should be stressed in promotion:

- Value for money
- Service levels
- Delivery schedules
- Product specification and design.

These are the messages which must be sent to customers. We suggest a variety of both above- and below-the-line promotional activities, including advertising in *Office Furniture World* and *Design for the Office*. Target audiences include architects, specifiers and company purchasing officers.

The most important element of promotional activity, however, should be personal selling. In particular the sales force needs to be retrained to stress value and to market economic value to the customer. In the long run we feel that this approach will pay off once again for Fine Furnishings Limited.

★ ★ ★ ★ ★

BUSINESS COMMUNICATIONS

Case 8.2: Dairy Slim

Answer

(*a*) Confidential report on new product development for the slimming market.

To: Mr David Forsythe
From: Student name
Date: 10 January 1995

1 Terms of reference

The research was carried out for us by XYZ Research Company from January to June 1993, among a sample group of 500 respondents aged 15–55 from ABC1 socio-economic backgrounds, male and female residents in Bristol, Manchester and London.

The research was initiated to identify, among our existing target market, the following:

* motives for wanting to lose weight
* methods for weight control
* foods which people dislike giving up.

2 Procedure

In-depth interviews were conducted in the respondent's home and responses recorded on tape by the interviewer. These were then interpreted by us from the analysis provided by the research agency as shown in the appendix.

3 Findings

3.1 Motives for wanting to lose weight

Respondents wanted to feel physically good and healthy (68 per cent and 67 per cent respectively), which were the highest scoring responses, followed by wanting to be fit (43 per cent). Being more attractive and popular (21 per cent and 15 per cent respectively) were the lowest scoring answer.

3.2 Methods for weight control

Thirty-two per cent felt that watching diet and intake were most important, followed by physical activity (22 per cent). Taking medication and stimulants was the lowest scoring method (3 per cent).

3.3 Foods which people dislike giving up

Thirty-one per cent disliked giving up cakes, pies and bakery products, followed by sweets and sugar (23 per cent), alcohol (17 per cent), meat (15 per cent), chocolate (13 per cent) and 9 per cent for each of cream, fruit juice, potatoes and pasta.

4 Conclusions

The majority of respondents wanted to lose weight in order to feel better, and tried to do so by reducing their food intake and taking more exercise. They particularly disliked giving up high-calorie foods and snacks.

5 Recommendations

On the basis of this research information I recommend that we should continue to develop foods which are low in fat and calories as substitutes for 'normal' foods which people like to consume, but which will also appeal to people who are not dieting as a healthy option; this could also be used as a theme in our communications and promotions campaign.

At present we specialize in dairy foods, but I recommend that we should consider diversification into bakery products and then, investment allowing, into the confectionery and sugar-based product markets to become low-fat/calorie food brand leaders.

(*b*) Graphic presentation of categories of research information

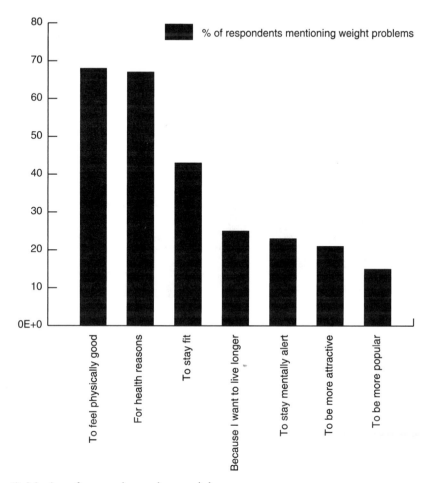

(i) Motives for wanting to lose weight

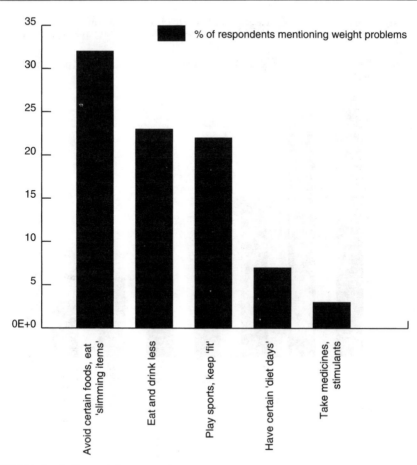

(ii) Methods for weight control

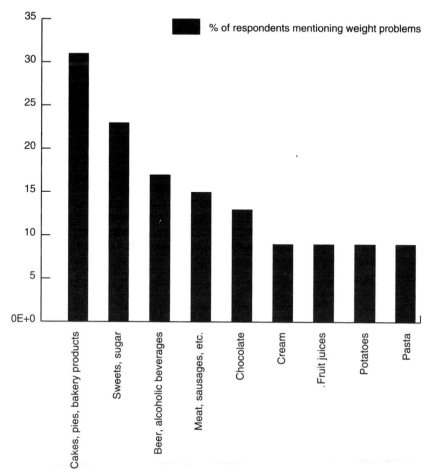

(iii) Foods which people dislike giving up

FUNDAMENTALS OF SELLING

Case 8.3: PME Ltd

Answer

(a) Memo:
   To: Sales Director
   From: Telesales Manager
   Subject: New products and new territories

The telesales operation has been able to produce a steady stream of orders because the items are 'low-ticket', i.e. order values are low. It would be unrealistic to expect the telesales staff to have any success at all in attempting to sell £3,000 items over the telephone, even though they are an experienced team.

It would be more realistic for the telesales operation to be used to generate qualified sales leads in the new territories, for the salespeople to follow up. In other words, our telesales operators would take enquiries that might flow in from any marketing campaigns that the company runs, and telephone the potential customer. The main objective of their call would be to set a sales appointment for the representative.

We might set as a secondary objective the gathering of feedback information for the marketing department.

I would also suggest that the telesales staff would need a full training programme on the new products, competitors' offerings and the nature and location of the target customers.

(b) By implication all of these salespeople have been operating in and around head office. Most of them are likely to be unfamiliar with the new territories in which they will be working. This will mean that much time will be wasted at first in becoming familiar with the geography, although a portable computer and geographic territory planning software would go some way towards mitigating this problem. The representative will also be unfamiliar with the subculture of the new area. There will be different accents, and perhaps different ways of doing business, and he or she will certainly have no business networks to plug into.

In addition, they have been used to selling what appear to be low-value, repeat order items. Now they are being asked to sell products that will in many case be capital purchases for the target companies. Different techniques and processes will need to be learned. It is also possible that a customer will only ever need one or two of the new products, so every sale will have to be a new sale, and not all of these leads will come from the telesales operation – many will have to be generated by cold canvassing.

(c) Salesperson _____

    Date of call _____ Time _____

    Client reference _____

    Result of call _____

Obviously, if the client places an order it should be reported in this section.

The salesperson will be the only face of the company that customers in more remote locations will see. It is likely, therefore, that the client will always turn to the representative for help and information. Customers close to a head office will often develop a number of close ties with various people in the organization. It is vital, therefore, that reports sent back from the field are comprehensive, detailing all requests and conversations between the salesperson and the client, on such matters as quotations, competitors' products, expediting delivery, technical queries and background information on the client company.

Competitor and market information

There may be competitors operating in a salesperson's territory who are unique to his or her patch. It is important, therefore, to relay all information about competitor activity as quickly as possible. In a similar vein, although the marketing department may have researched the area as efficiently as possible prior to launch, there is no substitute for accurate market information picked up on the ground.

Actions required

Here, any actions that the general sales office or other departments need to take should be clearly defined, also the intended date and purpose of any follow-up calls by the salesperson.

*   *   *   *   *

Case 8.4: Textbook quotes

Answer

(a) **Market segmentation**

The concept and techniques of market segmentation and targeting have for some time now been central to effective modern marketing.

Segmentation and targeting is the process of dividing a market into distinct subsets (segments) where each subset represents a separate market comprised of customers with similar needs and wants and who will respond to a particular marketing mix.

As suggested in the quote from Hammer and Champy, the idea of market segmentation developed from the attempts of earlier marketers, such as Henry Ford, to mass-market products. As consumers became more educated, informed and affluent, they gradually moved away from being satisfied with a mass-produced product identical to those purchased by their neighbours to requiring products and services which were more closely designed to meet their individual needs and wants.

Among the more common methods of consumer-market segmentation are:

- demographic methods: age, sex, social class
- geographic methods
- behavioural methods: product usage, product purchase habits, psychographic, etc.
- attitudinal methods.

Using one or a combination of the above factors, markets are broken down into subgroups where the consumers in each of these subgroups are grouped together and targeted.

In recent years increased competition, together with social and economic changes, has meant that these segments are now breaking down into smaller subsegments which in some circumstances may now be as small as the single customer referred to in the quotation. This means that increasingly many customers do require an individual approach and products and services which are suited to an individual taste. Clearly this poses problems for the marketer, as such 'customized' products are very expensive and, in fact, beyond the income of most consumers. However, developments in segmentation techniques allied to powerful consumer databases have allowed the modern marketer to come very close to targeting much smaller and often individual customer groups. The newer techniques of geodemographics such as Acorn enable the marketer to identify the needs of specific or at least small numbers of customers.

The mass market has indeed broken up into pieces, but the modern marketer can now cope with this targeting opportunity.

(b) **Knowing and understanding the customer**

It is true that the focus of the marketing function has changed from pushing products through aggressive selling to establishing what customers want and then satisfying these needs. Indeed, this is the essence of modern marketing. It is also true, as Pine suggests, that people do not like hard-sell tactics. The idea, however, of understanding the customer to such an extent that selling is superfluous is not without its practical problems. Below are some of the more frequently encountered problems in trying to understand customers.

Changing customer requirements

One of the factors that makes it difficult to understand customers fully is the fact that customers' needs and wants are volatile. Factors such as competitive innovation can serve as a stimulus to changing customer requirements, as can changes in the circumstances of the customer, such as financial status, family circumstances and so on.

This does not mean, of course, that it is impossible to understand the customer; indeed, it emphasizes the need for constant monitoring of customer needs and wants.

Inadequacies of market research

Although in general market research techniques are nowadays sophisticated and advanced there still remain many problems in conducting consumer market research, particularly in terms of predicting customer behaviour. Sometimes these stem from the limitations of the research techniques available, but in addition customers, when presented with hypothetical scenarios with regard to, say, future product purchase, will sometimes be less than honest about their real feelings, buying motives and future intentions.

Inadequacies of consumer behaviour theories

As with marketing research, concepts and models of buyer behaviour have improved considerably in recent years. As research has continued in this area, so our knowledge and understanding of this area of behaviour have been enhanced. However, the models available are still low on predictive power.

Certainly the marketer is now much closer to Drucker's claim that marketing should make selling superfluous, but even now our knowledge and understanding of customers is not so great that the product will sell itself.

(c) **Application to the public sector**

There is little doubt that the arguments advanced in both quotations apply very much to the public sector, including government departments and authorities responsible for the administration of local/municipal affairs.

In recent years we have seen the application of marketing concepts and techniques to a much greater extent in this sector. There are a number of reasons for this, including, for example, the opening up of public sector services to greater competition through, say, compulsory competitive tendering.

In the case of quotation 1, this has meant a move from the equivalent of Henry Ford's mass marketing to the segmentation and fragmentation of markets in the public sector. Customers in this sector also no longer behave as if they are all cast in the same mould, and increasingly demand products and services designed for their unique and particular needs. This means, of course, that the marketer in public sector settings must increasingly practise segmentation and targeting.

In the case of quotation 2, public sector marketing, although only relatively recently, has woken up to the importance and effectiveness of understanding customers. The practical outcome of this has been an upsurge in the use of marketing research tools and techniques, including customer surveys, focus groups and other marketing research techniques in order to evaluate customers' needs and wants. As in the commercial sector, it is unlikely that customers' needs and wants will ever fully be understood in the private sector, but the public sector marketer is now prepared and having to pay more than lip service to the understanding of customers.

★   ★   ★   ★   ★

SELLING ENVIRONMENT

Case 8.5: Newspaper articles
– Paints and the environment

Answer

(a) **Balancing legislative and economic forces**

Increasingly marketers have found themselves squeezed between having to comply with an ever expanding and complex range of legislation designed to protect and enhance the environment and the economic realities dictated by the law of supply and demand. Marketers must therefore learn to balance these legislative and economic forces. In order to understand the problems and concerns in achieving this balance we shall outline the issues facing a paint maker squeezed between two laws. We shall start by examining the law of the land which imposes ever stricter environmental controls.

(i) *Environmental controls*

In recent years, both in developed and developing economies, the marketer has been faced with ever increasing legislation regarding protection or enhancement of the environment. Initially a concern for the minority, so-called 'green' issues have become a concern for a large number of people, including consumers, economists, marketers and politicians. Green issues and legislation encompass a large number of diverse activities and areas which are important to marketers. Below are some examples of green issues which have prompted new laws on legislation:

- the 'greenhouse' effect due to depletion of the ozone layer
- depletion of scarce resources such as forests, minerals, etc.
- pollution of rivers and seas
- pollution of the atmosphere, acid rain, carbon monoxide, etc.
- illnesses caused by manufacturing and using products which contain toxic materials, such as VOCs in paints.

All of these and other areas of concern have prompted new legislation and stricter controls. Effective marketers have responded by seeing these concerns and controls as an opportunity rather than a threat, and have acted early to develop products and procedures which either comply with existing legislation or negate the need for new legislation. However, in many cases complying with the law of the land means higher costs and often higher prices. This brings the marketer into direct conflict with the law of supply and demand.

(ii) *The law of supply and demand*

The law of supply and demand is essentially based on balancing the use of scarce resources through the price mechanism. For example, price is used to equate demand with supply. In simple terms, at higher prices less would be demanded of a product or service, while lower prices will result in greater quantities being demanded. For the individual marketer, therefore, there are many advantages to keeping prices as low as possible. But this in turn requires costs to be low and, as we have seen, new legislation to protect the environment often results in higher costs and hence potentially higher prices for the marketer. This means that marketers need to 'sell' higher prices to customers based on the advantages of being more environmentally friendly. A problem in some markets, however, is that not all countries are as concerned about the environment, and producers in these countries can therefore often undercut the marketer who has to comply. This in turn can mean a loss of market share and profits.

We can see, then, that there are very real issues facing the paint makers described in the *Financial Times* article. The contemporary marketer must learn to balance the constraints of ever stricter environmental controls and the law of supply and demand.

(b) Main internal and external sources of data

The main internal and external sources of data which our industrial paint maker might use to identify sales trends over the past five years are shown below.

Internal sources of data

- Company sales records
- Company accounts
- Interviews/questionnaires with existing sales staff
- Previous research carried out by the company.

External sources of data

- Government statistical service
- Bank reviews
- Publications of the Market Research Society
- Digests, e.g. marketing yearbook
- Trade and marketing periodicals
- Published reports, e.g. Mintel, Euromonitor
- Chambers of Commerce.

We can see that there is a wide variety of sources available to an industrial paint maker to identify sales trends. In determining sources of data it is important to be specific about the precise types of information required. For example, is the information required on national sales trends or international sales trends? How detailed does the breakdown need to be?

In consulting external sources of data in particular, it is also important to assess the reliability and validity of such information before using it for decision-making purposes.

★   ★   ★   ★   ★

PROMOTIONAL PRACTICE

Case 8.6: After Eight

Answer

Report: Launch of After Eight 5-Pack
To: Marketing Director, Rowntree Mackintosh
From: Rowley Hill, Account Manager, JWT

Introduction

As the account manager responsible for the promotional campaign for Rowntree Mackintosh's new After Eight 5-pack, I have been asked to present a report covering the following areas:

Part 1: The potential target market for the 5-pack
Part 2: Recommendations on the inter-media selection and scheduling
Part 3: Guidelines on how public relations activities can be used to support the media campaign.

1 Potential target market for the 5-pack

As you are aware, effective target marketing is essential to the development of all marketing plans, but it is particularly important in planning the promotional element of the marketing mix. The target market to a large extent determines message selection; media selection and scheduling and the relative emphasis on the various elements of the promotional mix.

Ways in which the market for this type of product can be usefully segmented include one or a combination of the following variables, e.g.

- age
- socio-economic grouping
- geography
- life stage
- lifestyle
- gender
- purchase behaviour
- attitudes
- personality/psychographics.

With such a myriad of potential bases to choose from it is important to select those which are most meaningful and relevant to the particular product market. For the new 5-pack it is suggested that the following factors should be considered in making the final decision about target market selection:

- Brand values on the 5-pack should build on those already established for the boxed After Eight.
- It is vitally important to match the attraction of brand values to the target audience.
- Associations of elegance, sophistication and social status attract an ABC1 audience.
- The target market for the boxed and 5-pack products will vary in that essentially the boxed product appeals to the gift sector (this being reinforced in the current advertising for the boxed product). The 5-pack is intended to be an indulgence snack and the purchaser is also likely to be the consumer of the product.
- Whereas the boxed product is aimed at male and female ABC1 markets, the 5-pack is more likely to be targeted at females who are higher consumers of impulse confectionery products.
- The consumer is also likely to be an existing consumer of boxed After Eight who sees the purchase as a treat, reward or pick-me-up.
- In line with our earlier research, the age profile for the target customer is likely to be 25–44.

2 Recommendations on the inter-media selection and scheduling

As you are aware, media selection involves solving the problem of finding the most cost-effective medium to deliver the desired number of exposures to the target audience.

Among the key decisions in media choice are:

- selecting between the major media types
- selecting specific media vehicles and deciding on media timing and scheduling.

In turn these decisions, in addition to reflecting target market selection, must also reflect considerations such as budget, flexibility, overall marketing objectives and corporate and brand image.

It is suggested that bearing all these factors in mind the main media vehicle should be television. This should be a national TV campaign designed to support the roll-out of the product. Our media planning department confirms that this is the most cost-effective method of reaching the target audience on the basis of advertising exposure to target market. In addition, however, it is suggested that the television advertising be supported by a planned campaign involving the following other media:

- Women's magazines
- National press
- Posters
- Cinema.

In terms of timing it is important to achieve integration across these main media vehicles, and we shall be proposing a scheduling programme to achieve this. We are also suggesting that the budget be allocated in the first twelve months to a 50 per cent 'burst' spend during the first month of launch with the remaining 50 per cent being used to fund a drip campaign for the remaining twelve months. In addition to the media advertising, of course, we are also planning a sales promotion campaign aimed at both consumers and major retailers. Details of this will follow in a separate report. Finally, it is suggested that a public relations campaign be planned to support the launch of the product. Details follow in the final section of this report.

3 Guidelines on public relations activities to support the media campaign

To a large extent public relations (PR) has not been used extensively to support and promote individual brands. However, if planned and managed effectively, PR activities can be very useful in supporting individual products. It is, however, important that the PR campaign should be fully integrated with the above-the-line campaign. The following is an outline of the key considerations in planning an effective PR campaign for the 5-pack.

- Identification of relevant publics for PR.
- Identification of PR objectives.
- Planning and implementation of PR effort.

It is suggested that the following PR activities be used to support the media campaign:

Press releases (trade and national)
Product publicity
Corporate publicity.

As mentioned earlier, it is important that specific PR activities are planned to coincide with and support the new product launch campaign in the media. We suggest that the PR activities used to support the new 5-pack could include a charity balloon race, with product donations to local hospitals and a link to the activities of the Worldwide Fund for Nature.

More detailed plans for the PR campaign will need to be finalized with you, and we look forward to discussing the plans for these in the product launch in more detail.

* * * * *

MANAGEMENT INFORMATION FOR MARKETING AND SALES

Case 8.7: Bishop Business Publishing Ltd

Answer

Report: Marketing Strategy and Information at Bishop Business Publishing
       Ltd
To: Marketing Director, Bishop Business Publishing Ltd
From: P Boswer, Marketing Information Analysts Ltd

Introduction

On the basis of the preliminary information provided on Bishop Business Publishing Ltd, this report addresses the following areas:

Part 1: Possible courses of action for Bishop.
Part 2: Further quantitative and qualitative information required in order to make decisions regarding eliminating particular channels of distribution.
Part 3: How technology might be employed to assist the information needs of the company in the future.

Part 1 Possible courses of action for Bishop

1   The information provided pertains primarily to the volume of sales and respective costs, revenues and profit margins associated with the alternative channels of distribution. Clearly, before making any final decision with regard to eliminating channels of distribution further information will be required. This is a strategic decision and should not be taken on the basis of only partial information. Further information requirements, both qualitative and quantitative, are outlined in Part 2 of the report. However, on the basis of the information already available we are able to outline possible courses of action together with what we feel are some of the key considerations associated with each course of action.

1.1 Maintain existing mix of channels of distribution

In many ways this represents the easiest option. The current mix of 30 per cent wholesale, 50 per cent retail and 20 per cent direct means that Bishop is not over-committed to just one major channel alternative. In addition, although the use of intermediaries does obviously reduce both the degree of control which Bishop can exercise over marketing and profit margins per unit, it is important to remember that intermediaries do perform certain functions on behalf of Bishop. For example, the wholesalers break bulk and help reduce stockholding and distribution costs. Similarly, retailers often promote the books, again reducing overall marketing costs.

1.2 Increase wholesale and/or retail share of business: increase order size

This course of action would entail taking steps to reduce the direct sales business. Although at first glance at the costings shown in the cost structure table, this would appear to be a non-starter, in fact if Bishop were to attempt to increase average order size from the current 100 for wholesalers and 4 for retailers, this might significantly reduce total costs.

1.3 Increase direct sales

Clearly, this would appear to be the most attractive alternative on the basis of new receipts per book. In addition, this alternative allows us to increase the royalty payment per book to authors, thereby making Bishop more attractive as a publisher to existing and new writers. However, as with the previous two alternatives, it is very important to consider the effect on costs, revenues, profits and royalties per author of volume. Specifically, we need to remember that overall company profits are a function of both net profits per book *and* volume. Certainly direct sales are much more profitable per book – indeed, the net profit is actually £9.50 per book if we take account of the recovery for carriage. However, before taking a final decision to develop this method of distribution and possibly eliminate others we will need further information, both qualitative and quantitative, as shown in Part 2.

Part 2 Further information required

2   Before any final decision can be made to eliminate particular channels of distribution, further quantitative and qualitative information should be obtained. The main types of information needed are as follows:

2.1 Quantitative information

- Detailed sales quantities by channel.
- Total profit per channel.
- Analysis of how costs have been apportioned for each channel.
- Estimates of market size for products sold.
- Competitor market shares and sales by channel.
- Total national sales by each channel.
- Trends in growth or decline of each type of channel.
- Relationship between order size and costs of distribution.

2.2 Qualitative information

- How well the company's products are suited to each channel.
- How well the company's strengths match various channels.
- Distributor perceptions and attitudes.
- Customer perceptions and attitudes.

It is suggested that this information be collected via a formal marketing research exercise so that Bishop can plan its future distribution channels. A variety of research methods are advised, starting with secondary information from published sources and followed by a primary research exercise specifically to explore the qualitative issues. It is suggested that a series of focus group interviews involving samples of both distributors and groups of final customers should be used.

Part 3 Technology and future decision making

It is suggested that Bishop Publishing initiate a feasibility study for implementing new technology to assist marketing decision making in the future. It is envisaged that this would be part of a planned management information system. Such a system should utilize up-to-date technology to aid decision making. Examples of how such technology could help are as follows:

- Investment in computer technology could provide the firm with essential marketing information quickly (for example, spreadsheet models of sales and costs by channel).
- Similarly, computer technology could be used to build a customer database that can be used to secure higher profits by exploiting the most profitable channels.
- Computer-based modelling systems could be used to speed up planning and improve the accuracy of forecasts.
- Continuous updates and 'what if' questions may be answered using computers.

These, then, are just some of the ways in which technology could help to assist the company in the future. Generally speaking, computer-based information is now relatively cheap compared to only three or four years ago. However, as always with management information systems, speed, accuracy and the range of information need to be balanced against cost and improved decision making.

★   ★   ★   ★   ★

EFFECTIVE MANAGEMENT FOR MARKETING

Case 8.8: The Garden Design and Landscape Company

Answer

Report on marketing activities at The Garden Design and Landscape Company

(a) A more marketing-oriented culture

1 Background

- The Garden Design and Landscape Company is well established, operating in both consumer and business-to-business markets.
- Its marketplace is becoming increasingly competitive and the company is not doing as well, with sales conversions having fallen from 1:3 to 1:7.
- Faced with an increasingly competitive environment, management need to change the focus of their business, becoming more customer-oriented to ensure that resources are not wasted.
- The company is currently product-oriented so this will require a significant culture change.

2 Changing to a marketing-oriented culture

- Reorienting the culture of the company takes time, costs money and can be a painful process.
- It will only be possible if the change has the support of senior managers.

3 Proposals

- To review the current organizational structure, to consider a structure based around customer groups.
- A flatter structure with delegated responsibility and targets for work teams.
- To establish a system of improved management and marketing information, including marketing research to provide the basis for improved decision making and to ensure that future decisions are made based on customers' needs. To keep costs to a minimum, the first priority would be to review the current internal data and to identify ways in which these can be managed more effectively. The company has the advantage of knowing its customers by location, type of work required, order value, etc. and so is well placed to undertake fairly simple research in-house.
- To introduce a programme of customer care for all staff. This should be undertaken gradually using cascade training within the company to keep costs down.

- Management to be encouraged to consider going for a quality standard certificate such as BS 5750, although this will entail substantial cost so may be deferred for a year or so.
- Over the longer term to review the scale and organization of the sales and marketing department and consider appointing a marketing director.

4 Time scale and budget

Activity	Time	Budget
Review current organization structure	2 months	
Proposed and agreed changes with all staff	4 months	
Implementation of changes	3 months	
	Consultancy time – 10 days assuming no redundancies	£8,000
	Management time	30 days
Customer care training	Starting immediately with managers	
	1-day course for each work team of 10	
	Spread over 12 months	–
		£7,200 trainer costs
Review of internal data	3 months	20 staff days
		5 consultancy days at £4,000
Development of improved database and MIS	24 months	To be tendered
BS 5750	18 months from year 2	
Appointment of a marketing director	Year 2	Est. £40,000 salary 8 staff days + £5,000 selection costs

(*b*) **Improving the effectiveness of sales and marketing team**

- Review organization away from area sales offices towards customer segments.

Sales manager

| Corporate sector sales team | Domestic sales team | Public sector key accounts |

- Evaluate current customers to identify target segments.
- Use ratio analysis to identify strengths and weaknesses of current sales and marketing effort.
- Establish clear, realistic sales targets for each sector.
- Provide support to ensure maximum benefit of sales effort, e.g. telesales and direct mail, to generate qualified customer leads and follow up on enquiries.
- Establish a basis for monitoring performance of sales and marketing effort.

★   ★   ★   ★   ★

MARKETING OPERATIONS

Case 8.9: IKEA Furniture Retailer

Answer

(a) Defining marketing planning

Marketing planning is the systematic process of assessing marketing opportunities and resources, determining marketing objectives and developing a plan for implementation and control. Marketing planning involves the creation of a marketing plan, which may be short-range (one year or less), medium-range (two to five years) or long-range (over five years).

The need for marketing planning

Many of the benefits of marketing planning are self-evident and not particularly industry-specific. Applying marketing planning will help IKEA to do the following:

- Stay in touch with trends in the marketplace. Marketing planning hinges on analysing key trends and environmental changes so companies which use it tend to maintain awareness of what is going on.
- Ensure an understanding of customer needs. Marketing planning will require IKEA to regularly appraise and review key customer needs and how well they are being satisfied.
- Keep competitors under scrutiny. Competitor analysis is an important part of the process which IKEA will go through and should help the company understand the strategies and likely future actions of key international and local players.
- Develop strategies which target appropriate customer groups. The background analyses which have been carried out help identify the most suitable customer targets and segments where the greatest potential exists. By understanding its own strengths and weaknesses IKEA will also be able to understand the feasibility of particular actions.
- Put together appropriate marketing programmes (mixes) for targeted customers. The understanding of customer needs, competition and marketplace which IKEA has developed will help the company fine-tune its marketing mixes.
- Ensure the appropriate level of resourcing which has been developed with the particular strategies and programmes in mind.

(b) The relationship with corporate planning

Corporate planning is important in determining an organization's overall mission. It helps set goals which relate to all departments of the company, including R & D, engineering, production, finance, personnel and sales, as well as marketing. Corporate planning is therefore a plan of all aspects of an organization's strategy in the marketplace whereas a marketing plan deals with implementing the marketing strategy as it relates to the target markets and the marketing mix.

(c) Detailed marketing plans

Company mission

This is to offer a wide range of furnishing items of good design and function, at prices so low that the majority of people can afford to buy them.

Product/market background information

Here IKEA could review the nature of segmentation and sales within the market in which it operates. This could include an understanding of customer needs by segment as well as an appreciation of key operators within relevant target markets.

SWOT analysis

This is a review of IKEA's key strengths and weaknesses as well as the available opportunities and challenges which the company may be facing. While the strengths and weaknesses will be concerned with internal organization issues, the opportunities and threats will relate to conditions in the external environment. The details included will vary, but may include some of the following issues:

Strengths
- low cost base
- upmarket brand
- stylish Swedish image
- full range of furniture and furnishings under one roof
- good customer facilities
- self-service stores
- mass-market appeal
- provision of full colour catalogue.

Weaknesses
- out of town
- flat-packed items
- reliance on mass market

- need to keep prices low
- need to follow/set fashions.

Opportunities

- move into new geographic markets
- attract new demographic/psychographic groups.

Threats

- price competition from other multinationals
- local, more culturally tuned-in competition
- world recession and low consumer spending power.

Statement of objectives

These objectives will relate to what IKEA aims to achieve with its marketing programmes. These will combine general objectives, such as keeping costs low, maintaining service quality, finding simple solutions to problems with specific sales targets and expected results by target segments.

Strategies

These will be concerned with which target segments are under review, what the basis for competing (competitive edge) will be and how the offerings are to be positioned. For IKEA these strategies could be specified in terms of the customer targets, such as couples in their 20s and 30s setting up home for the first time and what is being offered to them, such as the stylish, sophisticated, Swedish, keenly priced product range.

Programmes

These concern the tactics in terms of products, price, promotion and distribution. For example, this will involve specifying the core global product range, as well as suggesting local additions to the portfolio. Given that IKEA falls roughly within the service sector, it may also be appropriate to consider people, process and physical evidence. For example, standard staffing levels, store layout, order processing systems, etc. are all part of the offering to be determined.

Allocation of resources/tasks/responsibilities

Making programmes happen involves the allocation of resources to a range of activities as well as determining the tasks and responsibilities which individuals, both centrally and locally, must carry out. For example, the global nature of the IKEA offering means that much promotional activity must be coordinated centrally.

Financial implications/budget

These include a breakdown of costs, estimates of sales and revenues and discussion of the expected return on investment of implementing the marketing plan.

Operational implications and implementation

Here any operational considerations associated with implementing the plan are reviewed. Measures of performance and ways of evaluating whether goals and objectives have been achieved are put in place. IKEA is likely to set these performance measures centrally and on a store-by-store basis. This will help identify under-performing areas.

Appendices

These provide any supplementary information which may support the arguments presented in the plan and help those preparing, reading and using it. For example, IKEA might include detailed sales figures for the last few years, which help marketers determine likely trends and make forecasts.

★ ★ ★ ★ ★

EFFECTIVE MANAGEMENT FOR SALES

Case 8.10: Chicago Mutual

Answer

To: Sales Manager, Chicago Mutual
From: Marketing Consultant

(a) **Mutual's commission structure**

1 Introduction

The total remuneration package offered to sales people may consist of a number of component parts:

(a) Basic salary.
(b) Commission/bonus.
(c) Car or car allowance.
(d) Expenses and other personal allowances, e.g. clothing allowance, preferential loans or low rates of interest, etc.

The ratio of basic salary to total potential earnings differs between industries and even among different firms in the same industry.

2 Current practice

(a) It is common practice within the insurance business that sales people are paid on a commission system only, with no basic salary or car/car allowance. Hence sales people are, to all intents and purposes, self-employed and paid *only* on results. If they do not manage to sell a policy or upgrade an existing policy holder, they receive no payment whatsoever.

(b) The philosophy behind such a commission structure is to keep the sales force on its toes and 'hungry' for success. The commission system is designed to ensure that individual sales people view sales success as an absolute necessity because, basically, if they do not sell they do not get any money to live, pay their mortgage, buy petrol, etc. The prospect of being without money to live on concentrates the mind wonderfully and acts as a strong propellant to increase effort. The stimulus to effort is basically fear; fear of failure and insecurity.

3 Implications

(a) While such a philosophy works in the short term, its long-term effects are open to question.

(b) Chicago Mutual has problems retaining sales personnel beyond an average employment time of six months.

(c) Even the best sales people owe it to themselves and their families to secure their futures. A commission-only occupation is an extremely precarious way of earning a living.

(d) A realistic basic salary would remove some of the pressure of insecurity, create a feeling of belonging to the firm and may well contribute to more good sales people remaining with Chicago Mutual for longer periods.

(e) Sales personnel are failing to get a sufficient amount of new business. Because the commission structure means they have to sell to live, it is probably perceived as being easier to make a secure income from servicing existing clients and getting repeat business or upgrading policies than attempting to gain new business.

(f) Servicing existing clients is of paramount importance in retaining and repeating business, but new business is necessary to offset cancellations and achieve constant growth (i.e. the sales manager's job depends upon producing an increase in premium volume in each six-monthly cycle).

(g) The best sales personnel are usually those with the most adept sales skills and who are capable of prospecting and generating new business.

4 Recommendations

(a) A differential rate of commission (i.e. a higher rate than repeat business or upgrading) on new business will encourage the better sales people to spend more of their time prospecting.

(b) The extra financial rewards resulting from the above will give better staff an additional goal to aim for as well as presenting them with a more challenging job. It will also act as an incentive for such staff to stay with the company.

(c) Training schemes should be devised to explain to new sales people that it is better to build up a solid customer base, because repeat business will bring greater potential rewards in the longer term.

(b) Importance of on-going training

1 Introduction

Induction training is an absolute necessity when a new recruit joins the sales team. Induction training should ideally include such things as:

(a) Product knowledge (including price).

(b) Company knowledge.

(c) Knowledge of systems and procedures.

(*d*) Selling processes and techniques.
(*e*) Knowledge of competitors.

2 Current situation and implications

2.1 New members of the sales team take some time to become useful and productive employees. Once hired, they spend two weeks in a training school to learn:
(*a*) Standard sales presentations,
(*b*) How to answer objections,
(*c*) Some knowledge of consumer and organizational buying behaviour.

2.2 This initial training session is the first and only programme of instruction in the whole of the sales person's career with the company. There is a great danger in viewing training as a necessary evil that needs to be dealt with as soon as possible, and as something that once it is over it is finished with. This view is myopic, to say the least, not to say naive and simplistic. Obviously the management of Chicago Mutual do not appreciate the concept that success comes through people. Training is not a 'one-off' thing to be 'got out of the way', but should be a continual process of personal achievement and adaptation to changing circumstances.

2.3 New sales recruits are given induction training in standard sales presentation techniques, but new techniques are being developed and circumstances change. New conditions in the external business environment may necessitate the use of a different approach and a different (not necessarily new) set of 'techniques'.

2.4 Customers need and want change in response to environmental changes. Different business conditions, adverse economic climate or other environmental change may give rise to different customer priorities, different reasons for purchasing or not purchasing and different reasons for objecting. A 'potted' course in the first two weeks is highly unlikely to equip the modern professional sales person with the knowledge and skills he or she will need throughout an entire career.

2.5 A final point relates to Chicago Mutual's high rate of staff turnover. Professional sales people want a career, not just a job. Many employees perceive regular training as a valuable thing. It assists them in personal development, job satisfaction and in obtaining promotion. Often posts without training are viewed as 'dead-end jobs', with no career path or scope for personal development. Introducing an on-going programme of regular updating training sessions may well contribute to retaining a higher proportion of good staff.

3 Conclusion

Success comes through people. Training is not a 'one-off' expense to get out of the way as soon as possible; rather it is an investment in human capital. Customer needs and wants and the general external environment are in a constant state of change. A one-off induction course at the start of a sales person's career with the company is inadequate. Training should be a regular, systematic and on-going process. Regular training results in a more adept and efficient sales team, a chance of personal development and hence greater overall job satisfaction and sales performance.

★　★　★　★　★

SALES OPERATIONS

Case 8.11 : Homeclean Limited

Answer

Report: Homeclean's proposed switch to more direct selling

(*a*) **Background**
This report considers whether Homeclean Limited is justified in engaging in so much above-the-line advertising, or whether it should engage in more direct selling. A number of assumptions are made pertaining to the position of Homeclean in the UK market and the performance of its range of products. The main assumption is that, although sales have been steadily increasing, the increase is not significant, and it leads one to ask the following key questions.

Is Homeclean sufficiently marketing-oriented?

1 There does not appear to be a strategic marketing plan.
2 Encouragement for expansion is coming from 'outside'. There is no evidence of research/market analysis.
3 Homeclean is paying 'lip service' to marketing and there is almost a total reliance on TV advertising.
4 There is no indication that the parent company is prepared to commit itself to the effective expansion of Homeclean (i.e. the establishment of manufacturing plants on the continent). This would not be supported on such a small domestic base.
5 Perhaps most importantly, where are the marketing audit and feasibility study on the European opportunities for the Homeclean range of products?

Arguments for more direct selling

There needs to be some consideration of the following:

• Who are our customers?
• Where are they?
• How do they buy?
• What products from the range are they buying?
• What is our price range?
• How shall we sell? How shall we distribute?

All these points give rise to concern, but the question that most needs to be addressed is: 'Why is an estimated 90 per cent of the advertising and promotional spend above-the-line?' The marketing mix is simply not balanced, and available resources are being misdirected.

There also appears to be a lack of synergy within Homeclean's operation, evidenced by the 'internal competition' method. Homeclean ought to consider more concentrated sales efforts within its own sales force. It should consider the effectiveness of utilizing intermediaries and direct its sales force efforts into a higher penetration of the retail market through a more concentrated approach to its distribution. There will need to be incentives in its channel to encourage intermediaries to extend their range of Homeclean products. The reliance on TV advertising is unjustified – mainly because such advertising may be directed at the wrong customers. More below-the-line activities are essential for Homeclean. A balanced proportion of spend should be used by the sales force, integrating efforts and efficiencies at the intermediaries in the channel to increase the market penetration and availability for the customer.

Conclusions

The company would be well advised to establish a more balanced marketing mix and a much stronger orientation on below-the-line activities aimed at the distributor and consumer, by diverting resources away from costly, often ineffective, TV advertising. It is quite clear that some effective research on advertising effectiveness is required, but there needs to be a move towards below-the-line activities such as in-store campaigns, leaflets and trade advertising in order to increase the presence of Homeclean in the marketplace.

(b) **Key considerations in switching to more direct selling**
1 There may need to be a change in the salesforce structure to implement and accommodate any such change in direction.
2 The marketing manager should review the marketing position of the company in liaison with the company management team and devise a marketing plan. The plan should form the basis of all future activities. As part of this plan, some key elements should emerge:
   (a) There is a need to establish a logical and disciplined framework for the planning process.
   (b) This must be underpinned with meaningful research.
   (c) The necessary steps must be taken to convert the items in the plan to actionable propositions on the ground.
3 There needs to be a quantifiable strategic objective. This may be to 'increase market penetration by 20 per cent by financial year end 1993 and to implement productivity and cost efficiencies in the sales structures on an on-going basis'.
4 There needs to be an effective market intelligence system which monitors sales promotional activities on an on-going basis.
5 Direct selling activities need to be implemented quickly and effectively. In addition, policies need to be sufficiently aggressive to have an impact

upon the market. There will, of course, be cost considerations, but in view of Homeclean's previous reliance on TV advertising the medium-term benefits of an aggressive direct selling approach would outweigh such costs.

The choice of the advertising agency

The more direct, strategic approach to selling which has been suggested may mean that Homeclean needs a new agency, especially in view of the potential expansion overseas. It may be that an advertising and promotions agency will be more effective, for the simple reason that it may be able to perform below-the-line activities to implement the coordinated approach to the strengthening of Homeclean's UK base. In considering the choice of advertising agency, Homeclean will need to consider:

* the previous performance of agencies
* the need for an agency which is familiar with several European markets. In particular, the agency will need to be aware of any social/cultural differences of countries within which Homeclean may operate
* submissions from agencies with bases in the UK and Europe in order to satisfy the demands of the parent company.

Conclusions

The switch towards a more direct selling approach from an above-the-line policy will require some radical alterations within Homeclean. The starting point, without doubt, is the formulation of a balanced marketing plan comprising effective use of resources. There needs to be careful monitoring of direct selling activities in order to improve methods and, finally, careful selection of an advertising agency to ensure that any expansion within the UK and Europe is coordinated and planned.

* * * * *

11 Diploma level: mini-case specimen answers

Case 9.1: The Mondex Card, electronic wallet

Answer

Report: Recommendations for Marketing Communications Strategy for Mondex Test Market and Roll-Out
Prepared for: National Westminster Bank and Midland Bank
Prepared by: A Marketing Consultant
Report date: January 1994

(a) Problems that marketing communications strategy must address

The following are felt to be the key problems:

- New technology is involved.
- There will be customer and trade resistances.
- The project involves many organizations.
- A great deal of education of both customers and trade will be required.

Using the simple AIDA (Attention, Interest, Desire, Action) model the chosen marketing communications must deal with:

- increasing awareness of what the system will do
- developing interest in the benefits
- stimulating desire to register as a user
- creating action to use the system.

(b) Alternative marketing communication activities

A greenfield situation exists. Therefore it is important to consider all the alternative methods of marketing communications either in the context of the test market or of the national roll-out programme.

Limiting factors will be the availability of media in Swindon.

The size of the promotion budget.

The identity of the target audiences indicated by the initial research.

It is likely that a complex mix of methods will be used, including:

* advertising – to reach wider audiences
* public relations – because of novelty/newsworthiness
* direct marketing – use banks' customer database
* sales promotion – at the point of usage (retailers/banks)
* signage – 'use your Mondex here'.

(c) **Recommendations on strategy**

* Develop strong brand image
* Maximize on PR potential
* Develop high-impact local press advertising
* Direct mail bank customers
* Personal selling to retailers to encourage take-up
* Wide availability of literature
* Freephone number for information
* Tracking research to monitor.

(d) **Means of measuring effectiveness**

* Levels of take-up, number per 1000 of population
* Number of transactions
* Freedom from difficulties/complaints
* Measurement of attitudes and awareness
* PR coverage in the media.

(e) **Implications for roll-out nationally and internationally**

* Learn lessons, modify branding or message if necessary
* Consider further test region
* Consider television advertising
* Test market in another country (after one year's operation)
* De-bug the system
* What about fees for users of the system
* Improvements in technology.

These, then, are my views regarding a marketing communications strategy for the Mondex test market and roll-out. I look forward to discussing these with you in more detail.

* * * * *

Case 9.2: The Ash Grove Kindergarten

Answer

Report: Marketing Communications Plan for 1996
Prepared for: Mrs Lorna Ash
Report date: December 1995

1 Overview of the current situation

1.1 It is understood that you are making a substantial personal and financial investment.

1.2 Year one is predicted to make a small loss (£2,500).

1.3 Despite a flood of enquiries from prospective clients, actual starts for January are insufficient to fulfil forecasts.

1.4 The financial situation is likely to get worse unless further action is taken to generate and convert enquiries.

2 Marketing communications problems

2.1 As no history of success exists, Ash Grove Kindergarten has no word-of-mouth recommendations. You must therefore establish an awareness and sound credibility base for the organization, its people and its products.

2.2 There is a need to define clearly the prime motivation to register among defined target market groups to ensure that communication activity meets defined needs. It may be that the original forecasts were too optimistic and that numbers will only build up slowly. Product positioning may need to be adjusted.

2.3 With the present economic situation unlikely to help in attracting placements, it has perhaps the advantage that unemployed people may be available to help.

2.4 A specific problem is communicating on a limited promotional budget with limited knowledge of the marketing communications business. You will need to renew priorities for a communications action programme in relation to the target market groups to be exploited.

2.5 Clearly break-even volume is important, i.e. the high fixed costs, and this will determine the scale of the task.

3 Marketing research proposals

Before proceeding with the design and development of the communications plan, it is recommended that the following research be conducted:

(a) to provide a database;
(b) to provide a benchmark for subsequent research initiatives.

3.1 Key buying motives

I suggest you talk to parents who have signed up to find out why.

3.2 Reasons for non-take-up of registered places

The research here could be conducted among parents who have made enquiries but did not sign up, to find out why not.

The research need not be costly and you could carry it out yourself within a week by telephoning the target groups. Analysis of the responses from the different groups will indicate the nature of the marketing communications task to be undertaken, and from this a budget level can be proposed to achieve the communications tasks specified.

4 Communication objectives

- To create a sufficient level of awareness of the kindergarten.
- To differentiate the kindergarten from the competition by stressing quality and value for money but avoiding the 'air of exclusivity' if the research findings indicate this would make it more accessible.
- To gain the reputation of being well run.
- To generate more enquiries.
- To encourage a positive attitude towards registering.
- To ensure that communication activities are integrated and effective in reaching the target audience.
- To select appropriate marketing communications media to reach the identified target audiences.

It is important that your investment in promotion is regarded as a capital investment and that you integrate the communication activities into an effective plan. The timing of marketing communications requires sustained communication *immediately* and *over the next twelve months*.

5 Target audiences

Originally:

(*a*) middle-class professional parents
(*b*) employers of these executive parents.

Wider target market groups:

(*c*) Single mothers
(*d*) Job sharers
(*e*) Part-timers.

The communication activities should:

- target corporate clients specifically
- widen the geographical base.

6 Communications programme

The results of the research will indicate the purchase motivations for each target market group. You should concentrate on using the most effective medium to reach your target audience. It is likely that an integrated programme will be the most effective, and the following elements are likely to be important.

6.1 Personal selling

To both individual and corporate clients. It is likely that this activity will take up much of your time. You will need to follow up the flood of enquiries by telephone inviting prospective parents and employers to visit the kindergarten.

6.2 Direct marketing

Leaflet target areas. Establish a database to capture, for example:

- members
- enquirers
- health visitors
- opinion leaders
- local nursery schools
- mothers mentioned in birth columns.

Offer member incentives – get another to register.
Obtain a list of health visitors/opinion leaders and mail them an invitation to visit.
Contact the local nursery schools – get them to recommend Ash Grove.

6.3 Above-the-line advertising

- Regular advertising in appropriate local papers
- Posters in doctors' surgeries (with permission)
- Advertisements in the National Childbirth Trust regional magazine.

6.4 Below-the-line sales promotion

- Opening offer – discounts for two children
- Discounts for prepayments
- Special schemes for companies
- Offer special services with a defined radius – pick-up/drop-off.

6.5 Public relations

- Planned events and news releases
- Regular newsletter for parents and prospective parents.

6.6 Launch day itself – 4 January 1996

Maximum use must be made of free media exposure and PR should be used to achieve this.

Opening by a local celebrity known and loved by three- to five-year-olds. The target should be to get coverage by local papers and local radio, even regional TV (if you have a contact). Provide information pack for editorial use.

On the launch day, offer:

- free badges
- balloons
- car stickers ('I've been to Ash Grove')
- information pack for parents.

7 Monitoring and controlling the plan

- Monitor where enquiries are generated
- Measure conversion rates
- Research awareness levels to monitor changes
- Carry out customer satisfaction surveys
- Monitor competitive activities
- Review and revise plans as progress and/or changes are made.

8 Budget

8.1 Clearly, the promotional expenditure needs to be planned. Initially this is likely to be high in order to establish a reputation.

8.2 Total cost of promotion to date – £4,000. This should not be regarded as a one-off payment.

8.3 You should concentrate initially on low-cost methods as outlined in 6 above, with specific emphasis on personal selling and public relations.

8.4 Each new child raises £3,000 (60 × 50 weeks).
Total capacity = 60 children × £3,000 = £180,000 per annum.
Taking 10 per cent promotional cost:

£18,000 per annum = £1,500 per month.

It would be reasonable to spend up to £1,500 per month until total capacity (60 children) is reached.

* * * * *

Case 9.3: The Big Cat's on the prowl

Answer

Effective international Jaguar brand promotion 1995–1999: Presentation notes

Prepared for: J. Walter Thompson Advertising Agency
Prepared by: Marketing Communications Manager of Jaguar
Report date: January 1995

1 Marketing analysis/objectives

- Ford are new owners.
- Have set volume target of 100000 by year 2000.
- To be achieved by:
  - £700 million new product development
  - wider model range
  - international expansion
  - increased product benefit
  - broadened demographic appeal (younger drivers)
  - integrated marketing communications.
- The principal objective is to achieve the growth target through the above strategies in a highly effective, international brand promotion.
- Other objectives are:
  - to increase awareness levels in the AB, 30 to 50 years old target group, principally male customers
  - to reposition the brand within the core markets of the USA, UK, Japan and Germany
  - to develop customer loyalty programmes
  - to prepare for the launch of X200 in 1998
  - to sustain the marketing communications budget at a rate of 5 per cent of total sales.

2 Positioning and targeting

Critical qualities

- traditional
- high-quality, high-performance
- successful brand, successful owners

- male AB, 30–50 age group
- accessible price
- high augmented value, warranties
- range from driving enthusiasts to chairmen.

3 Strategy and tactics

Engage a broad but integrated marketing communications campaign.

- *Direct marketing*
  Develop and strengthen customer loyalty and satisfaction among core groups. Continue after-sales communications.
- *Advertising*
  Select media range to fulfil awareness thresholds. Develop a media theme which is creative and memorable. Advertising will be carried through to international markets.
- *Public relations*
  There is a wide range of publics: own staff, distributors, suppliers, motoring journalists as well as users and potential users. Jaguar has newsworthy stories and must gain favourable publicity.
- *Motor shows*
  Attendance at international motor shows is essential. This is another opportunity to generate customer enquiries.
- *Sponsorship*
  Jaguar will maintain its sports sponsorship and seek to develop brand perception of success, performance and international competitiveness.

4 Media selection

- *Press*
  Both national quality newspapers and specialist car magazines are the preferred media. Care should be taken in selecting appropriate international equivalents due to language and differing brand perceptions. Target media could include Amex/Diner's Club members' magazines and yachting and golfing magazines.
- *Television*
  Is expensive but has high impact and could be used at launch periods.
- *Radio*
  Although a car, especially Jaguar, has a high visual appeal, a radio commercial can transmit performance data and augmented benefits. Selected commercial programmes with high AB awareness could be employed, i.e. Classic FM in the UK.
- *Posters*
  Highly visible and cost effective but requiring careful choice of appropriate sites. Could also be used at specific launch periods.

The above main media will, of course, be supported by PR, sponsorship, exhibitions and quality literature.

5 Creative rationale

Critical qualities to be included in the creative work have already been described. In addition, the following elements are important:

- *Colour*
  The Jaguar green should be predominant as it conveys traditional qualities.

- *Logo*
  The Jaguar logo is highly visible and very well recognized.

- *Themes*
  Quality, tradition, performance, success.

- *Lifestyle*
  Feature successful people – 'achievers' with younger image.

6 Budgets/scheduling

	1995 £m	*1996* £m	*1997* £m	*1998* £m	*1999* £m
Advertising					
• UK core market	3.0	3.5	4.0	4.5	5.0
• USA/Japan/Germany	6.0	7.0	8.0	9.0	10.0
• New market entry	1.0	2.0	3.0	4.0	5.0
Total advertising	10.0	12.5	15.0	17.5	20.0
Direct marketing					
• UK	0.3	0.4	0.5	0.5	0.5
• International	0.3	0.6	0.9	1.2	1.5
Motor shows	3.0	4.0	5.0	6.0	7.0
Public relations	1.0	2.0	3.0	4.0	5.0
Sponsorships	1.0	2.0	3.0	4.0	5.0
New product launches	1.0	2.0	3.0	4.0	5.0
Total	16.6	23.5	30.4	38.7	44.0
Contingency fund	1.4	2.5	2.6	3.8	4.5
Total promotion	18.0	26.0	33.0	42.5	49.0

7 Monitoring and evaluation

The key means of monitoring overall success will be the achievement of sales targets and associated profit and growth targets. Market share statistics in specific sectors will also be monitored.

Specific promotional components may be monitored by other appropriate means, including:

- *Advertising* Brand recall and attitudes to Jaguar.
- *Direct marketing* Number of enquiries generated.
- *Public relations* Favourable editorial coverage.

* * * * *

MARKETING COMMUNICATIONS STRATEGY

Case 9.4: Dennison Aggregates

Answer

To: Account Director,
          ABC Business-to-Business Advertising
From: Marketing Manager,
          Dennison Aggregates

Marketing communications brief for new product 'RRM'

1 Remit

You are hereby requested to produce a costed campaign plan for launch advertising directed at the construction industry. The aim is to create a favourable environment in which our sales force can convert latent demand into actual sales. Your proposals are required for presentation to a marketing planning meeting to be held on 3 July.

2 Background

2.1 The new product

Our research and development people have developed a mortar mix, codenamed RRM, which can be delivered to construction sites ready-mixed in purpose-designed containers of 0.3 cubic metres capacity, weighing 50 kg, that can be either forklifted or crane-slung to the point of use. They can be delivered within 24 hours of ordering, and the mortar remains workable for 36 hours thereafter. RRM is intended for large-scale brickwork applications.

2.2 Market research

Representative samples of builders' merchants and building contractors in two major centres of construction activity were recently interviewed by telephone. The market research company's report, included as an appendix to this brief, shows that contractors react very favourably to an explanation of the product but that merchants would be reluctant to stock it. It was also found that the former typically expected a price of £3 per bag, while the latter could only be persuaded to reverse their negative reaction at a buying price no higher than £2. These perceptions combine to produce a 33 per cent margin on sales for merchants. We can achieve target profitability by supplying the product at those prices (assumption).

3 Current situation

3.1 Product profile

The basic product specification is given in 2.1. The fact that it is ready-mixed saves labour on site but, more significantly, overcomes at a stroke the quality control disadvantages of the traditional mixing method: bags of cement, pile of sand, labourer, shovel and cement-mixer. The dimensions of the container make it possible to get mortar in bulk to cramped or high sites, overcoming equally dramatically the familiar problem of wheelbarrowing manageable quantities more or less continually.

The product is clearly capable of delivering significant benefits to both contractors and merchants, which need to be communicated clearly and persuasively. It offers on-site labour saving, quality control and bulk handling advantages to contractors, who will no longer have to allocate scarce site space to the stockpiling of sand and cement. It is a clean and convenient product for merchants, who can order it day by day for delivery the day after and thereby enjoy quick and profitable stockturn.

Your short-term communication strategy should use these undoubted benefits to stimulate the desire to try the product. We invite your advice on the appropriate development of that simple strategic aim in the longer term.

We have no plans to offer the product to the do-it-yourself domestic market at present (assumption).

RRM is ready for full commercialization immediately. No competitor is yet in a position to come to market, as far as we know.

3.2 Company profile

Our view of the way the company should present itself to the market has not changed since previous briefings. In the case of the RRM campaign, there is a particular opportunity to position the product as an important technical advance from the research and development programme of a manufacturer with a reputation for innovation, which pioneered the generic product fully thirteen years ago. It must be crystal clear that RRM comes from a division of a major national quarrying group, so that any 'mad scientist' undertones are cancelled out by the message of size and solidity.

3.3 Audience profile

The market research report introduced in 2.2 shows that one target audience is exceptionally receptive to the product idea, commenting that building contractors' responses to attitude-scaling questions produced average scores 'among the highest and most uniform' in that company's experience over the last eight years. We can expect many of them to behave as classic 'innovators', while most of the rest will be readily converted 'early adopters'.

The other, equally significant, target audience is, unfortunately, sceptical. Builders' merchants in the survey typically interpreted 36-hour retardation in terms of shelf-life and foresaw order scheduling difficulties. They believed that RRM would appeal only to the smallest contractors and the do-it-yourself market. The market research report concludes that they will 'wait for demand to materialize rather than take the initiative'. The challenge in this case will be to convince 'laggards' of the benefits the product can deliver to them.

There is some hope that demand from contractors will pull supply through the chain and confound the merchants' pessimistic response to the hypothetical questions of the survey.

3.4 Pricing policy

We are preparing cost breakdowns and alternative pricing strategies for the launch, within the general parameters set by contractors' and merchants' expectations. These will be available to you in time for price to be built into the communication strategy if appropriate.

3.5 Distribution policy

Our own vehicles will deliver from quarries and regional depots. Computer-controlled scheduling will ensure that 24-hour delivery is achievable as routine even during the peak periods in the industry. Buyers will be able to place their orders centrally at a Linkline telephone number. The containers will be returnable against a deposit, the exact amount yet to be decided (all assumptions).

4 SWOT analysis

4.1 Strengths

- First to market
- Unique product
- Clear user benefits
- Rapid response delivery
- No change required in distribution logistics
- 36-hour workability
- Contractors' price expectations favourable
- Merchants' price expectations can be met.

4.2 Weaknesses

- Relatively narrow market segment
- Indifferent merchants
- Radical challenge to normal working practices
- 36-hour retardation cannot compete with on-site storage of unmixed ingredients.

4.3 Opportunities

- Capture whole market before competition materializes
- Establish high profit margins
- Improve standards industry-wide
- Enhance Dennison's reputation
- Establish RRM as the generic product.

4.4 Threats

- Merchants' obstinacy
- Labourers' fear for jobs
- Union disapproval of innovation
- Consequent delay gives reaction time to competition.

5 Objectives

The primary aims of the campaign in the first year will be to achieve:

- 100 per cent awareness within both target audiences
- trial among 70 per cent of building contractors in the target audience
- trial among 40 per cent of builders' merchants in the target audience
- sales of five million containers.

Secondary aims will be to enhance our corporate image, reinforce staff morale and gain favourable publicity beyond the primary target audiences for the campaign. We seek your advice on appropriate ways to quantify such objectives and thereby measure the extent to which they have been achieved.

6 Strategies

6.1 Budget

Although subject to parent company approval, the suggested budget for marketing communications expenditure this year is set at 10 per cent of last year's sales revenue, producing a budget of £4 million in round figures. No more than a quarter of that sum can safely be allocated to RRM (assumption). Your proposals for above- and below-the-line spending and all agency fees must be contained within this target.

6.2 Marketing communications mix

Your recommendations are required on the most cost-effective allocation of effort above- and below-the-line and the most appropriate balance between supply push and demand pull, firmly grounded in your business-to-business advertising expertise.

If exhibitions feature in your plan, it will be important to distinguish users from specifiers (such as architects or local authority planning officers) among the visitors and perhaps to target these influencers if the budget permits.

The fact that we have well cleaned and closely targeted mailing lists already available will presumably favour some form of direct marketing activity. We shall certainly need sales promotion and sales support materials in time for the start of our new product field force training programme.

As an innovation, RRM has clear publicity potential. A programme of press releases and publicity events is required. Live demonstrations such as bricklaying competitions might be appropriate for the peak launch period.

6.3 Creative brief

'RRM' is only a codename, of course, and your recommendations are required for a brand name that has immediate appeal, is self-explanatory, conveys the innovative nature of the product and will defy 'me too' variations by competitors. Proposals should be prepared for application of the brand name to packaging and labelling, conforming to the Dennison house style within which you have worked before.

Where advertising is concerned, we shall expect the usual creative rough treatments to be presented for approval at an early stage.

6.4 Media brief

We look to your expertise in business-to-business communication for a draft media plan, justified by good evidence of the coverage and readership of the proposed vehicles, a clear statement of the position and environment of our campaign and a cost-effectiveness analysis of various options within a general plan.

7 Schedule

Scheduling of the whole marketing communications strategy will be a particularly crucial consideration because the construction industry is highly seasonal. Your advice on precise starting dates for all above- and below-the-line campaigns will be essential, within the general constraint that headquarters has just made the decision to go to market and will be anxious to see some progress sooner rather than later.

8 Implementation

At this stage, responsibility for development of the campaign will lie at divisional director level. All planning meetings will require the attendance of an account director from ABC (yourself, I hope) and the Dennison divisional sales and marketing director. Decisions with strategy implications will require board-level approval on both sides.

Thereafter, operational control will be in the hands of your designated account manager and myself, while strategic decision-making authority devolves from board to divisional level on the Dennison side.

9 Campaign evaluation

We require costed recommendations for an appropriate procedure to check and amplify the findings of our limited telephone research survey (see 2.2) while campaign development is proceeding.

You should also propose a rigorous programme of post-tests and tracking studies, capable of measuring performance of the campaign against objectives (see section 5) at key stages, with costs. It would be particularly useful to be able to make judgements about the relative cost-effectiveness of the discrete campaigns within the total marketing communications strategy. We shall monitor sales trends as usual, to assess progress towards the achievement of our fourth objective.

Budget allocations will be released at intervals, phased with the continuous research programme, so that tactical adjustments can be considered as necessary to achieve campaign objectives.

10 Action

Your preliminary response to this brief is required for a progress meeting here on 1 July. The agenda will be:

(*a*) Agree campaign objectives
(*b*) Confirm pricing strategy
(*c*) Confirm budget and time scale
(*d*) Discuss your campaign plan
(*e*) Decide next actions.

Please let me know as soon as possible if any further information is vital at this stage.

Donald Black

★　★　★　★　★

INTERNATIONAL MARKETING STRATEGY

Case 9:5: Star Engineering

Answer

(a) Control and marketing implications of world leadership plans

1 Introduction

Star Engineering is currently a medium-sized manufacturing company which is actively seeking to increase both market share and market coverage in specific worldwide industrial markets. The company has developed steadily over a number of years, progressing from a traditional exporting sales approach to international sales offices and a distribution centre.

2 Future plans

Star Engineering has a corporate objective of worldwide leadership. This is a challenging objective. The time span for its achievement is long-term, say ten years. A number of different routes, including international manufacturing and perhaps joint ventures and alliances, might be required to enable the world Star status to be reached.

3 Strategy

Careful consideration must be given to the strategic issues of how Star will achieve world leadership. Both product development and market development will be needed. Expansion within Star's existing markets needs to be considered. It is probable that the UK market share of 65 per cent will need to be defended vigorously. The important positions gained in the Middle East and South East Asia should be considered for further growth.

Market development into new country markets will be a key strategic area for Star. The major markets in the world need to be identified and decisions made about the suitability of market entry. The significance of the world triad of the United States, Japan and Europe cannot be ignored. Past decisions to avoid the German and US markets needs to be challenged in the light of the new corporate objective.

4 Organizational control

4.1 The main issue facing the management of Star Engineering is whether to maintain full control of all company activities from the UK headquarters or whether control should be decentralized to various countries and regional and continental groupings.

Inevitably the organizational structure of Star will need to undergo significant change and development in order to meet its stated commitment to world leadership. The current organizational structure will need to change, perhaps in several stages, to strengthen the international/world focus and to increase the degree of expertise and involvement in the major markets for Star's products. For example, the organization could be separated between the UK market, a South East Asia division, a Middle East division and a 'new countries' division (perhaps Germany or the USA). In the longer term, mechanisms to coordinate different markets will be needed. In the short term the UK head office will remain the central focus of the company, but each division will have delegated authority for business and marketing in its own area. An important point to note in such a structure is the coordination and cooperation of each division and the UK head office to ensure that corporate objectives are considered and met.

4.2 The cultural implications of organizational change

The changes proposed for Star in terms of its organizational structure represent a major cultural change for the company. The company will move to being committed and being heavily involved in international business, and as such its employees will need to be prepared and developed to cope with and contribute towards the new focus on international business. The local ethnocentric view will be replaced by an international outlook. Each employee will be part of a 'worldwide' organization as opposed to a 'British' company.

5 Marketing implications

5.1 The marketing focus and operation will also change dramatically during the process of increased international involvement. Under the proposed organizational changes the marketing of Star Engineering will no longer be strongly centrally controlled. Rather each division (i.e. the UK, South East Asia, etc.) will carry out its own marketing programme with budgetary and strategic planning control being exercised in the UK headquarters. This reflects the need for adaptation in each area of involvement and the need to assist the process of improving customer relationships. It was seen in Singapore that the establishment of the distribution outlet helped greatly in terms of Star's customer orientation. This will be emphasized further in the new international moves.

Further details of the increased international involvement will be examined through the four Ps of the marketing mix.

5.2 Distribution implications

A variety of options is open to Star Engineering in addition to its existing methods:

1 Licence
2 Contract manufacture

3 Joint venture or other forms of alliance
4 Wholly-owned subsidiary.

Star must evaluate the risks involved, particularly in the high-cost/high-risk foreign direct investment decisions. Successful companies need to achieve internationally competitive cost structures. To gain this position Star will need to look at the lower cost countries for some of its manufacturing and product sourcing.

The distribution network must offer Star significant coverage of its potential market and give high levels of customer service. This will be particularly important in the US and German markets, if entered, because of the high levels of competition and because of the recognized high expectations that buyers have of their suppliers in these markets.

5.3 Product implications

Technical standards vary in different countries. Star must be aware of the main standards and be recognized in these standards in their major country markets. If the cost and operational implications of this are high, there will be major strategic choices to be made upon which standards to concentrate. Some standards and technical capability might need to be gained through acquisition and/or joint ventures and alliances.

The posture of the world leadership implies that Star will invest in R and D and will be developing innovative and relevant engineering solutions to customers around the world.

5.4 Price and promotion implications

Legal requirements relating to tariffs and technical standards will influence price, as will competitors and Star's marketing objectives in different markets.

In achieving world leadership, Star will need to develop a corporate personality that adds value to its products and services around the world. Decisions will need to be made on the suitability of the Star name and logo for extension to world markets. Progressively the company will need to use trade exhibitions, public relations and targeted advertising to reach its specialized business markets in different countries.

As can be seen, Star Engineering has many aspects of change that it must encompass in order to fulfil its corporate aim of world leadership. A further example of this will be the need for internal communications among its growing numbers and diversity of employees, in different countries, from different cultural backgrounds and engaged in a variety of tasks. Without care Star could grow, but fail to achieve cohesion. It might thus fail to convince world customers of its major status because the Star people are unaware of Star's importance.

(*b*) Approach to evaluating existing and new overseas markets

1 Introduction

An approach which can take account of the current position of Star Engineering is to look at market attractiveness, given the corporate long-term objective of world leadership, and to take account of the existing and potential business position for Star.

2 Factors in evaluation

Market attractiveness can be evaluated by market size, market growth trends, market profitability, the vulnerability of the market to competition, barriers to market entry and economic and political influences on company assets and the repatriation of profits. The business position of Star can be assessed through estimates of obtainable market share, return on capital employed, company sales and company profits.

3 Current position; existing markets

The current position for Star Engineering is that 62 per cent of its sales come from the UK, 21 per cent from South East Asia, 10 per cent from the Middle East and, presumably, 7 per cent from the rest of the world. In the answer to (*a*) we have already identified that strategically it is probable that the UK position will have to be defended and the South East Asia and Middle East position will have to be expanded.

Star should develop its marketing information system in these existing markets, especially in South East Asia and the Middle East. In particular, Star needs to track competitors and to distinguish between those operating within one (or a few) country market(s) and those international companies selling in a number of countries. An attempt should be made to view whether each company is operating country by country or whether it has a more coordinated international marketing approach. Such competitors would challenge the emerging Star Engineering and its world Star aspirations.

Star would need to scan the external environment, but because it is already marketing within the country it will be able to put the information into an appropriate economic and business setting. It needs to identify the profit potential within its existing markets. If it is proposing to commence manufacturing in a country, the high levels of risk need to be minimized by a much more detailed country evaluation of political, economic and financial factors.

4 Approach for new markets

In approaching new markets, Star Engineering needs to establish suitable countries to enter, those to avoid at all costs and those to enter with caution. The company must carry out a comprehensive low-cost scan to identify market attractiveness and the probable Star Engineering position within those markets. Initially the company is looking for published secondary data to give indications of size, trend and stability in country markets. However, it is likely to find that market statistics for Star's part of the engineering market are not readily available or are, perhaps, subject to considerable margins of error. It is difficult, therefore, in new markets to evolve marketing plans unless more detailed market assessments are carried out. The extent of the country market evaluation needs to take account of the importance of the market and the degree of financial risk to the company. In the more detailed country analysis, using methods to collect primary data, Star Engineering would need to use a marketing research agency with expertise in business-to-business markets and capable of operating in international markets.

The corporate aim of Star Engineering drives it to search for major new country markets, while needing to safeguard its existing markets. The type of engineering markets in which Star is operating means that secondary data sources are unlikely to be particularly specific. The evaluation of markets will therefore rely on secondary data sources to cover SLEPT (Socio-cultural, Legal, Economic, Political, Technological) factors and primary data sources for significant risk product markets. The evaluation approach used for the new markets should be based on the lessons learnt from the existing markets. The marketing information system for existing markets should be extended to give an increasingly complete world coverage.

★   ★   ★   ★   ★

INTERNATIONAL MARKETING STRATEGY

Case 9.6: *Leisureworld Bicycles*

Answer

Report on International Marketing at Leisureworld
To: Leisureworld's Board of Directors
From: Acme Consultancy

1 Introduction

Leisureworld is facing more difficult market conditions in the late 1990s than it has over the past fifteen years. The recent recession and the resultant over-supply of bicycles in the developed Western economies has made it more difficult to increase the current demand of about £40 million (1995).

2 Need for segmentation

Based on the information supplied and our discussions with you, we propose a more focused approach to the diverse markets for bicycles, through the use of market segmentation. The use of market segmentation will enable a more customer-oriented approach to each market and its needs, and supply a competitive edge to Leisureworld offers. We should thus be able to increase the efficiency of our marketing efforts when they are more precisely aimed and tailored to specific segments of (potential) customers who share certain characteristics that are significant in marketing terms.

There are many approaches to market segmentation. The one we propose below clearly identifies a group of substantial and accessible markets which exhibit a need that Leisureworld can satisfy. By focusing your marketing effort on these countries you should improve substantially sales to these markets, subject to economic factors (such as possible continued recession in some countries). In exploiting such markets, the opportunity to market other Leisureworld products through similar distribution systems or to similar customers should be taken, thus avoiding an over-reliance on the bicycle market.

3 Segmentation proposal

We propose to start the segmentation exercise by drawing a matrix which links the two main parameters of demand – the ability to purchase, as measured by level of economic development, and the need satisfied, as measured by the use for which the purchase is made. This results in the following table.

Economic development/need satisfaction criteria

Level of economic development	Use situation				
	Transport	*Leisure*	*Fitness*	*Racing*	*Play*★
Less developed					
Early developed					
Semi-developed					
Fully developed					

★ Includes children's bicycles.

We can now place countries in one or more cells in the matrix according to the degree of substantial demand based on a particular type of usage and the level of economic development. Where actual data are available through your own or trade sources, the actual percentage of the market for each category should be stipulated, together with the estimated market size.

We can now proceed to filter out those countries which, for various reasons, may be unattractive. Thus in a particular segment those countries whose market size is too small can be eliminated. Similarly, segments which are not leisure oriented (the company mission) can be ignored.

4 Justification

Leisureworld's mission is based on leisure, and your main competitive advantage is that of keen pricing based on global flexible sourcing. You can build on this strength by focusing your market efforts on those countries which are sufficiently developed to have a substantial leisure segment. Given the set-up and running costs in a particular market, it should be possible to calculate a minimum market size for a country to be viable in profit terms to Leisureworld.

Besides the infrastructure for cycling and the wealth to pay for leisure bicycles, it follows that such markets will also be viable for other leisure products. Similarly, the level of economic development almost certainly ensures a well-developed distributive and retail infrastructure, allowing Leisureworld access to the customers.

The one assumption we have made is that such customers will be receptive to low-cost leisure bicycles. As a market develops and matures, the major purchasers are the 'late majority' who, while desiring the product, are more cost-conscious than the fanatical early adopters. It is therefore likely that the markets identified will be in the early stages of maturity and thus likely to be more receptive to low-cost alternatives.

5 Communications and the cycle racing team

Given the international nature of Leisureworld Bicycles, an important consideration of any sponsorship must be the international appeal and application of any communication expenditure.

Any promotional vehicle used by the company needs to be adaptable and capable of being 'rolled out' in the form of a fully integrated communications package that will make a fundamental contribution to company objectives of:

- building a positive brand image based on the Leisureworld name
- adding significantly to market share by producing significant sales growth.

In particular, it is essential that Leisureworld Bicycles gives careful attention to the advantages and disadvantages of heavy investment in the cycle team. A full cost-benefit analysis should be carried out taking the criteria below into account.

5.1 Advantages of sponsoring the cycle team

- The Tour de France is an event of international significance. Its activities and media coverage are European-wide – a key market for Leisureworld. The intense media coverage – especially if the team were successful – would bring associated publicity benefits to the company and its products.
- Sponsoring the team would allow the company to feature specific personalities in the team and add character endorsements to the product range and brand. Quality, professionalism, toughness and style would be the characteristics transmitted via appropriate media placements, visits, endorsements, competitions, etc.
- Core viewers/audiences for cycle sports undoubtedly form a substantial part of Leisureworld's key markets – particularly in the sport and leisure segments. Moreover, even young children are influenced by successful sports persons, e.g. the recent Nike campaign.
- Racing does lend itself to an integrated campaign. The events are both geographically dispersed and spread out over a wide time period. Key events like the 'Tour' tend both to concentrate on key markets for Leisureworld (Europe 88 per cent) and to be timed at peak purchase periods (early summer in Europe). The use of endorsement, sales promotion and advertising can enable the interest to be maintained well into the other key buying period of late autumn (for the Christmas/children's market).
- From a defensive point of view, the absence of Leisureworld from such key events would leave other competitive sponsors in a very strong position regarding image and brand awareness that could leave Leisureworld having to rely exclusively on price to market its bicycles.

5.2 Disadvantages of sponsoring the racing team

- Concentration on one vehicle for promoting the brand constrains both the direction and flexibility of any communication strategy. In particular, the schedule of races would determine to a large extent the timing and location any promotion. Careful research would be required to establish the degree of 'fit' between the team's activities and the purchasing decision patterns of Leisureworld's diverse markets.

- There is also some doubt as to the degree of cross-market transferral of image that takes place, from the predominantly sports-centred racing team to other segments such as leisure and children's markets.
- In some cases the images of speed and risk suggested by cycle racing may be counter-productive in markets where safety is a key buying criterion.
- If the team should perform badly or get a bad image, this may reflect on Leisureworld – as in the Pepsi/Jackson fiasco.

6 Exploiting the team sponsorship

Assuming that Leisureworld goes ahead with the sponsorship, the following integrated communications plan is proposed:

- Agency selection would be a critical first step. Such an agency should have European-wide resources to cover the Leisureworld key market. A thorough knowledge of the industry and its markets, combined with a creative approach to bicycle marketing, would be essential.
- The initial campaign should cover the key periods from July to December and would most likely involve the following elements:
  - Sponsorship and public relations events centred around the team. Public appearances, product endorsements and opportunities for team members to 'champion' the brand should be created.
  - The development of a definite Leisureworld logo and style should be carried through to the team clothing, equipment and bicycles, and act as a house style for advertisements and point of sale materials.
  - The use of brand extension to cover cycle clothing and equipment via team endorsement should be exploited both in the bicycle market and in the leisure clothing market in general.
  - The use of competitions and gifts based around the team can be utilized to continue to build brand awareness and interest.

* * * * *

Case 9.7: Teesside Electrical

Answer

To: Bill Murphy, Export Manager, Teesside Electrical
From: International Marketing Consultants
Date: June 1995
Subjects: Forthcoming fact-finding mission; selecting trade fairs; other elements of the promotional mix.

1 Introduction

Before specifying countries, it is important to understand the methods by which we make our decision. A thorough analysis of Teesside would reveal a company with export success but with a limited knowledge of buyer behaviour in markets other than the UK. The company needs to find significant sales and profit growth in export markets. Teesside cannot visit more than a few markets; therefore secondary data must be used to screen the less promising ones. A more careful review needs to eliminate further countries from the list. The fact-finding visit is part of the information collection phase. The later stage of country selection and market entry will rely heavily on the information collected in the fact-finding mission. By the very nature of such missions, the data collected will be partial, biased and subjective. However, real qualitative insights can be gained.

2 Choice of countries

I recommend that you visit:

- Sweden and Denmark
- Germany
- France
- Italy
- Czechoslovakia.

As these are small markets in terms of the turnover you receive from them I can only assume that you do not have a resident sales person in each. I have therefore assumed that there will be sales persons located at the head office who make planned sales visits where necessary.

I suggest that the appropriate sales person accompany you to the appropriate country as they will be more familiar with the markets and will be able to advise you about the prevailing business and social culture and other matters.

3 Justification

3.1 Germany, France, Italy and Denmark

I have recommended Germany, France and Italy because you already have a presence in these countries. They are members of the European Union (EU), and as such have been subject to the same technical standards from January 1993. (In practice, many standards in technical areas have not been harmonized – much work needs to be done, and negotiations completed.)

You should visit building contractors who are already your customers. You must attempt to explore the relationship, to delve into their needs, wants and benefits sought. We need to find out how they see the development of our markets.

You will also be able to visit local government offices to introduce yourself, to gain information and also to make them aware of Teesside Electrical. Local governments influence public procurement; this has been particularly significant post-1992 with the new 'no home buying only' rules in force.

Your job will be easier in these three countries because you have past performance records to refer to and you already know who the main competitors are. Perhaps you need better information on their activities. What parts of the marketing mix do they emphasize?

3.2 It appears that you do not have any existing customers in Denmark. The ease of access may enable you to develop a niche opportunity.

3.3 Sweden

Sweden is a member of EFTA shortly joining the EU, and as such shares the trading benefits of the EC and EFTA market. It is possible that your products might meet the Swedish technical standards.

3.4 Czechoslovakia

This country has been selected because it is thought to be one of the most advanced of the old COMECON bloc. In the rapid change from a centrally planned economy to a market forces economy there could be market opportunities for Teesside.

4 Selection criteria for trade fairs

The following should be taken into account:

- How long has the trade fair been established?
- What is the reputation of the trade fair in our industry/target customer groups?
- Is the timing of the trade fair appropriate?
- Will the trade fair satisfy your objectives, and have you the resources in terms of time, money and personnel to exhibit effectively at the chosen fair?

It is important to collect as much information as possible to make the 'best' decision. Reputable trade fairs publish statistics on attendance, with breakdowns into sub-groups. The list of companies exhibiting in the past will give some impression of relative importance for your purposes. It should be possible on the fact-finding mission to cover the area of trade fairs. When visiting companies, the trade fairs visited and their value could be covered. It would be useful to check with the Chamber of Commerce and the Export Service of the DTI – the British Overseas Trade Board (BOTB) – to see what information they have on trade fairs.

While trade fairs are thought of primarily as a promotional tool, the opportunity to use the trade fair to collect information should not be neglected.

5 The other elements of the promotional mix

Teesside have a limited budget, are operating in new market areas and are operating in a complicated business-to-business market.

It is important that promotional activities are integrated and take account of the trade fair choice and timing.

The issues of language and appropriate communication for each relevant business culture must be addressed.

5.1 Sales force

The sales force can be used much more effectively than at present. In the less important markets, sales visits are only made when necessary. This might indicate to existing customers that their interests and their market are not really very important.

It is recommended that when you have established your key markets a small sales force is set up on the market area. This will enable you to attack the market much more aggressively.

In order to minimize cultural difficulties, it is suggested that a mix of Teesside expatriots and nationals is employed. This, if handled carefully, will give a good blend of language, culture, Teesside culture and product knowledge. It will be important to select nationals who have a good knowledge of the customer base in the chosen market.

In the lightning protection market the sales force will be most important in communicating and persuading companies unfamiliar with Teesside to buy. The sales force will have a large part to play. In addition, they will contribute significantly to the success of the trade fair.

5.2 Public relations

There are public relations opportunities, particularly regarding press relations, to communicate with the various target markets. Often trade fairs represent a focus of media interests. We should take this opportunity. We should, in addition, consider the range of stories that we can communicate concerning appointments, contracts won and technical development. We should consider a wide approach, not just press relations. Do we need to develop good contacts with the government and the public sector? What images are important for us?

5.3 Sales promotions

We should use appropriate business-to-business sales promotions. We need to establish the range of legally and culturally acceptable sales promotions in each market. Certainly we know that price discounting is likely to be important. We might find that special training programmes on 'the theory and the latest approaches to lightning protection' at one end of the market and on practical cost-efficient methods of fixing lightning protection onto buildings at the operative end of the market will give us some leverage.

5.4 Sales literature

Technical literature and company image literature is important in this market. It is crucial that reliable translations of all relevant material are made into the appropriate languages. Translations must be carried out by technically qualified nationals and should be back-translated to eliminate errors. It is also crucial that our translated material is available for the trade fair and before entry into each key market.

We must take great care to develop the right material. Our UK approach might not be appropriate for other markets. The balance of image promotion and technical factual material must be checked.

5.5 Advertising

It is likely that advertising will be the least important part of the promotional mix. If advertising is considered, it should be restricted to the key trade journals appropriate to our target group of customers. Bearing in mind the cost and importance of the trade fair, this should give the timing focus for advertising.

5.6 Summary

Selling will be the main part of our promotional approach. The trade fair, selected after considerable debate, gives an important focus to our European programme. This fair attracts buyers, in our market area, from most of our identified new key markets. Public relations will not be ignored, nor will sales promotion.

Our limited expertise in the new market areas will cause us to place considerable emphasis on languages and understanding the culture. We need to find ways of coordinating our promotion in various markets. Should we take an adapted approach for each market, should we aim for a completely or partially standardized approach?

* * * * *

INTERNATIONAL MARKETING STRATEGY

Case 9.8: Giant's Castle Games Ltd

Answer

From: L. Hardaker, Senior Consultant, Globe Planning Ltd
To: Andrew Marsden, Giant's Castle Games Ltd
Copy: Chris Culley
Subject: Outline of key strategic international marketing decisions 1996–2001
         Implementation of selected decision
Date: December 1995

1 Background

Following our recent discussions concerning the importance of the non-UK market and your objective to expand into international markets, we have, as requested, prepared an outline of what we suggest will be the key strategic decisions in international marketing which Giant's Castle needs to take over the next five years.

In addition, and again as requested, we have identified one of these decision areas facing Giant's Castle for a more detailed analysis and have developed a structured approach showing how this decision should be implemented.

Both strategic decisions and implementation issues have been set in the context of Giant's Castle's corporate and marketing objectives for the future, and the list of bullet points developed at your earlier meeting with Chris Culley.

2 Key strategic decisions

Entering international markets is an extremely important and potentially far-reaching step for any company. Because of this, it is important to approach this step in a systematic and planned way. The following are the key strategic decisions which Giant's Castle will need to take to cover its first five years of operation in international markets.

2.1 Establishment of objectives for international marketing

Although not strictly a strategic decision as such, the first step in planning for the future in any market, and, indeed, the background against which all strategic decisions need to be taken, is the establishment of clear objectives which are to be achieved.

Having familiarized ourselves with the situation of Giant's Castle, including an analysis of your current resources and corporate objectives, we suggest that the following be the objective which guides your international marketing plans for the next five years:

> To achieve sales in international markets representing a minimum of 50 per cent of current turnover by 1998, these sales to be achieved by developing primarily the European and North American markets.

2.2 Country selection

Although our suggested objective specifies that international sales growth is to be concentrated on European and North American markets, clearly these are very large and diverse markets. A key strategic decision, therefore, will be the selection of specific countries within Europe and selected regions in North America, which are to be selected as market targets by Giant's Castle. As a relatively small company new to international marketing you cannot hope, and, indeed, it is not desirable, to attack the whole of Europe and North America. All the evidence points to the fact that companies which focus on relatively few, carefully selected international markets fare better than those which spread their resources too thinly.

We suggest that initially you restrict yourselves to selecting two key European countries, together with Canada, as your target markets for the first two years of your international marketing plan. Market coverage can then gradually be widened on a roll-out basis as your experience increases and as sales and profits permit. Obviously market research will need to be carried out in order to identify which markets/regions offer the greatest potential and should therefore be targeted. Factors affecting this choice include size and growth of market, strength of competition, customer and market requirements, etc.

2.3 Method of entry

This strategic decision involves determining how the target markets selected will be penetrated. In part, this decision is related to the selection of objectives outlined earlier. Broadly, methods of entry can be divided into production in the home markets, together with either indirect or direct exporting, or the establishment of production overseas. Examples of specific methods of entry include an export management company, piggy-backing, using foreign distributors or agents, licensing, joint ventures and so on. Clearly, the range of alternatives is wide, and many factors will need to be considered in selecting a method of entry. However, as you know in your business, you need to persuade the 'publishers' in your selected overseas markets to accept your games. They, in turn, can reach the games console manufacturers. Initially we would suggest an indirect method of exporting, with a view to eventually establishing your own overseas marketing subsidiaries in selected European and North American markets. The aim would be gradually to increase control and involvement in your selected international markets over the five-year period of the marketing plan.

Because of the importance and potential complexity of the method of entry decision in international marketing planning, this is considered in more detail later in this report.

2.4 Marketing mix strategies: degree of standardization

The next key strategic decision – or rather, set of decisions – concerns your marketing mix for international marketing. Just as in domestic markets, you will have to make decisions concerning products, prices, place and promotion. Of these, we would suggest that product decisions will be central, with the rest of the mix decisions emanating from this area of the marketing mix. Examples of some of the strategic product decisions you will need to take in the context of your five-year marketing plan will include product range/ types, e.g. you will need to decide whether you intend to follow the games formula and/or take a new route into more interesting and 'involving' products. Central to decisions regarding the marketing mix, but again particularly relevant to the product area, will be the issue regarding the degree of standardization. At one extreme you may decide to produce standardized products both for home and all export markets, while at the other, you may decide that products will need to be adapted for each overseas market. Again, a large number of considerations will affect this standardization decision, but a central focus will be the potential trade-off between customer/market needs and cost/revenues.

2.5 Customer groups

In addition to selecting countries on which to focus your marketing activities, within each country decisions will need to be made concerning customer groups which you wish to target. Specifically, of course, you will need to determine which games console manufacturers and others to concentrate upon.

2.6 Other strategic decisions

We have outlined what we feel are the core strategic decisions in international marketing that Giant's Castle needs to take over the next five years. In addition, however, you will also need to take decisions in the following areas:

1 Organizational structure
2 Methods and sources of marketing research
3 Recruitment and selection of new personnel.

Although these are essentially supplementary to the key strategic decision areas outlined here, they are nevertheless crucial to the long-term success of Giant's Castle in international markets.

3 A structured approach to implementing the method of entry decision

As discussed earlier in this report, a key strategic decision area in developing

international marketing plans at Giant's Castle Games Ltd is the method of
entry decision. In this part of the report we have explored this decision in
more detail and suggested a structured approach to making and implementing this decision.

3.1 Alternative methods of entry

Below are shown the major alternative methods of foreign market entry.

Home-based production   Foreign-based
                                         production

Indirect export   Direct export
– Trading company   – Agents   – Contract manufacturer
– Export management   – Overseas distributors   – Licensing
  company   – Overseas marketing   – Assembly
– Piggy-back   subsidiary   – Joint venture
  operation   – Full ownership

As you can see from this list, there are a large number of alternatives for
foreign market entry, although the nature of your product means that
decisions about home versus foreign production are perhaps less critical
compared with other manufactured products. Nevertheless, the range and
complexity of entry decisions, together with the fact that decisions in this
area entail long-term commitments for Giant's Castle Games Ltd, means
that this is a crucial decision. Therefore care should be taken to ensure that
the decision is structured and implemented in a systematic way. We shall
start by outlining the key factors that will need to be taken into account in
making the decision.

3.2 Key factors in entry decision

- *Company-specific factors*
  In particular, corporate and marketing goals, size of company, desired
  level of involvement.
- *General factors*
  Number of markets being considered, legal and regulatory requirements.
- *Control required*
  The extent to which control over the marketing mix is desired will affect
  the mode of entry decision. More direct involvement equals greater
  control.
- *Incremental costs*
  The different methods of entry give rise to different working capital
  requirements. This is clearly important to Giant's Castle Games Ltd.
- *Profit potential*
  Long-term sales and costs associated with each method of entry need to be
  considered.
- *Investment requirements*
  Again, this is likely to be a crucial consideration for Giant's Castle.

- *Administrative and personnel requirements*
  The different methods of entry give rise to different administrative require-ments. For example, licensing often requires little extra administrative work for management. Similarly, one must also consider personnel needs.
- *Risk*
  The level of risk associated with international marketing varies with mode of entry. Not only commercial but also political risks should be considered.
- *Flexibility*
  Last, but by no means least, you need to consider how flexible are the different modes of entry. What might seem a suitable method of entry in the short term may be less so when considered over your five-year planning period.

These, then, are the factors that need to be considered in this area of strategic decision making. Ideally, for a systematic approach to making a choice of method of entry it is a good idea to use a scoring and weighting system for evaluating the different methods. You can start by weighting each of the factors outlined here according to their importance to Giant's Castle. Each of the modes can then be scored, say out of ten, to give an overall score.

You will need further market research in order to assess these modes of entry, and we shall be glad to advise on this. We appreciate that you are anxious to develop your international marketing, but we advise caution. First you must select your target markets, followed by a full evaluation of the different modes of entry. We suggest a minimum of four months for this. Once you have decided the mode of entry, you will then be in a position to recruit and select staff, change organizational structures and negotiate any contracts.

We look forward to our next meeting in order to discuss these issues in more detail.

* * * * *

PLANNING AND CONTROL

Case 9.9: Anderson Marine Construction Ltd

Answer

To: Senior Management, Anderson Marine Construction Ltd
From: J. Stacey, Marketing Manager
Report: Outline marketing plan for AMC new product range; methods of overcoming problems of implementation

1 Introduction

The reader should recognize that this is an *outline* of the marketing plan for a new range of boats and, as such, identifies a series of issues without necessarily addressing each in depth. The final and detailed plan can only be produced after further research has been conducted; the areas in which this research is required are referred to in the appendix.

2 Structure of the plan

Background
Situational analysis
Strategic imperatives
Principal assumptions underlying the plan
Preliminary marketing objectives
The target market
Positioning statement
The marketing mix
Implementation and control
Budgets
Appendix: areas for further research.

3 Background

The recent report submitted by the marketing consultant has highlighted the gravity of our current position and the need to adopt a proactive stance by developing a new range of boats which will broaden our trading base and reduce our vulnerability to the downturn in the custom-built and high-price sector of the boat market. With the board having accepted this recommendation, this plan outlines the steps that must be taken to ensure that the new range is developed and launched in time for the forthcoming selling season.

4 Situational analysis: a review of the business environment and the company's internal operations

4.1 The business environment

Market demand for medium-sized high-performance powerboats and yachts is currently depressed, with sales having dropped steadily over the last four years. Despite a series of price cuts, demand for our products has not risen and this, plus other evidence, suggests that the market is not price-sensitive. Instead, levels of demand are determined by more fundamental factors, such as levels of confidence in the economy. Economic and industry forecasts indicate few signs of an upturn in demand in the premium-priced sector of the market over the next two years. Anecdotal evidence and casual observation suggest that our competitors are similarly affected.

By contrast, demand for lower-priced boats currently appears to be rather more buoyant, with forecasts indicating that sales patterns in this area over the next few years are likely to be relatively stable. A larger number of firms operate in this part of the market and a greater emphasis upon prices and costs is inevitable. Preliminary evidence does suggest, however, that with careful positioning scope exists for AMC to establish itself in this part of the market.

(Note: These points are summarized as a series of opportunities and threats in the SWOT analysis.)

4.2 Strengths and weaknesses

4.2.1 Strengths
- Well-established manufacturer of high-quality and high-performance yachts and powerboats
- Loyal and knowledgeable customer base
- Financially successful
- Skilled workforce with a strong craft orientation
- Reputation for quality and performance.

4.2.2 Weaknesses
- Reactive selling approach
- Absence of a proactive marketing culture
- Recent reductions in margins
- Absence of a formal distribution network
- No previous presence or experience in the lower priced and higher volume sectors of the boat market
- Little experience of advertising and promotion
- Workforce with a strong craft orientation and little experience in volume production
- Seemingly little emphasis upon cost control and working to a particular price

- Delivery schedules.

4.2.3 Preliminary assessment of strengths and weaknesses

Although the company undoubtedly possesses a series of strengths, questions must be raised about the management's ability to capitalize upon these in the short term on entering the higher volume sector of the market. It is therefore essential that attention be paid to the issues of managerial expertise and culture so that gaps might be filled and a more proactive approach developed. Equally, the workforce has a tradition of producing high-quality products, but little real experience of volume production in which a strong adherence to cost control is fundamental.

4.3 Opportunities and threats

4.3.1 Opportunities

- Market and sales growth
- A reduction in the firm's exposure to one sector of the market
- Scope to capitalize upon the firm's reputation for quality and performance.

4.3.2 Threats

- A greater number of competitors
- The difficulty of establishing a worthwhile market position
- Possible problems in establishing a firm presence within the distribution network.

4.3.3 Preliminary assessment of the opportunities and threats

Our ability to capitalize upon the opportunities which undoubtedly exist in the higher volume sector of the market will depend to a very large extent upon our ability to move along the learning curve. The threats identified, while significant, are very largely predictable. Again, our ability to cope with these will depend upon *how* we move into the market and our ability to establish a distinct presence in the short term.

5.5 Strategic imperatives arising from the SWOT analysis

Given the nature of the findings of the SWOT, it is essential that we address several issues in the immediate future. These include:

- the skills gap in the workforce
- the absence of proactive marketing skills within the firm's management
- the development of an appropriate distribution network
- the development of a communications programme
- the financial implications of the proposal.

5.6 Principal assumptions underlying the plan

A number of assumptions underpin this plan, the most significant of which are:

- Demand for the current range will remain depressed
- AMC will be able to establish itself profitably in the new target sector
- Sales within this sector will continue to improve over the next twelve to eighteen months.

5.7 Preliminary marketing objectives

- To capitalize upon AMC's current very strong reputation by developing a new range of smaller and lower price of boats offering higher performance levels than the competition
- To position the new range as *the affordable high-quality small yacht and powerboat range*
- To achieve a distribution covering of x per cent (note that this figure can only be finalized in the light of further research)
- To achieve sales in year one of ___*, in year two of ___*, and in year three of ___*. These will translate into the following market share figures:
  Year one _____
  Year two _____
  Year three _____

* Again, these figures can only be determined in the light of further research.

8 Target market

A considerable amount of research is still needed to clarify the size and detail of the buying patterns of the target market (see appendix), and at this stage it is therefore possible only to provide a broad picture of the market. In essence, however, the range is designed to appeal to sailing enthusiasts who have several years of experience and who now wish to buy a boat which offers greater performance, albeit within a relatively restricted budget.

Given this, and as the consultant's report has highlighted, the market will require:

- a greater degree of active selling by the distribution network
- delivery from distributor's stocks
- exposure to an advertising campaign to raise levels of awareness and interest.

9 Positioning statement

The new range will be positioned as '*the affordable high-quality alternative*' in the mid-priced sector of the market. In achieving this position, full emphasis will be placed upon the broad values and heritage of our traditional range. The selling propositions will reflect both the performance of and linkages with our current range.

10 The marketing mix

The product range will consist of:

- Small high-performance yachts and boats that reflect a high value for money offer.
- Initial distribution will be through a carefully selected number of existing boatyards throughout the south, south-east and south-west of England. In the light of our experiences in the first year, consideration will be given to broadening this network in years two and three. Distributors will be selected on the basis of their:
  - current image
  - ability to provide sales and technical support
  - current sales levels
  - geographic location
  - existing franchises.

Emphasis will be placed upon the development of long-term relationships with distributors, with this being reflected in the high levels of marketing support provided by AMC and the margins offered.

- Prices will be set at the upper end of the sector in order to reflect the brand values associated with AMC, the quality of the product and the product's performance.
- Advertising and promotion will give prominence to the links with the existing range and will concentrate initially upon creating high levels of awareness and interest among the trade, the media and the target customer groups.

11 Implementation and control

Responsibility for refining and subsequently implementing this plan will rest with the marketing manager, reporting in to the main board. Given the significance of the proposed development, it is essential that the necessary levels of resources and commitment are allocated to the project. Control will be achieved through monthly and quarterly reports with a series of measures of performance against target.

12 Budgets

These will be set in the light of the findings of further research. At this stage, however, it is possible to indicate several areas of major expenditure, including:

- modifications to the production facilities

- the recruitment and/or retraining of the workforce needed to produce the new range
- the development of an appropriate distribution network, including funding of stock levels
- the funding of the principal dimensions of the marketing plan, including the advertising and research that will be needed.

13 Appendix

Areas of further research

In order to prepare a detailed marketing plan, a substantial amount of additional information is needed. Included within this is information on:

- accurate and detailed sales forecasts for the short and medium term
- the financial implications of the proposed action
- competitors: who they are, their size, location, patterns of ownership, resource availability, model ranges, strengths and weaknesses, selling propositions, positioning strategies, levels of advertising, pricing strategies and patterns of distribution
- customers: probable size of each market sector, geographic location, buying motives, sailing skills, approaches to buying and expectations regarding sales support, price sensitivity and readership profiles
- distribution: major patterns of distribution network currently in existence, locations, distributors' selling skills, levels of sales support needed, and expectations regarding levels of inventory, terms of payment, margins and advertising support needed
- trade shows: their relative importance, location, costs of appearance, visitor patterns and levels of media coverage
- media availability, areas of specific interest and copy dates.

14 Overcoming organizational problems of implementation

Given the nature of the business in the past, and in particular the relatively informal approaches to marketing that have predominated, I would anticipate a series of problems in implementing a plan which not only targets a new and very different set of customers from those served previously but also reflects an infinitely more proactive stance. For convenience, these problems can be categorized on the basis of whether they are essentially internal or external to the company. Those that are internal are concerned primarily with issues of culture, expertise and resource allocation, while those that are external are largely concerned with areas such as customer perception, the nature of the distribution network and the responses of those companies with which AMC will now find itself competing.

Beginning with the internal problems, the most immediate of these is likely to be the question of how best to develop a culture which is more suited to dealing with a higher volume and less specialized market than the one with which AMC has previously been concerned. Because AMC will still be producing boats for its traditional market and cannot afford to compromise its methods of operating within this sector, it may well prove to be appropriate to split the company in such a way that scope exists for a clear focus upon each of the two sectors. Assuming this is done, there will then be a need to begin the process of developing a managerial culture that gives full recognition to the rather different long-term development of the business. It would appear that the current workforce is heavily specialized and, assuming this to be the case, a degree of retraining and/or recruitment will be needed in order to ensure that the firm has the production skills needed for the new range.

At the same time, a rather different set of selling and marketing skills will be needed in order to develop the new product, launch it onto the market and subsequently ensure its success. A question therefore needs to be raised about the ability of the current management team to do this. Where gaps exist, and from a distance it seems most likely that these will be in the market and sales development areas, expertise will of necessity have to be recruited.

Other internal problems that are likely to be encountered include:

- whether AMC will have sufficient production capacity and flexibility
- identifying new suppliers and hence implementing a rather different purchasing policy from that of the past
- controlling costs rather more tightly. Given the nature of the comments in the case, it appears that price has not previously been a significant issue. Because of this, it seems likely that elements of tight cost control will not have been important. The new product and market will, however, demand a different approach if the venture is to prove profitable
- the development and cultivation of new and possibly tighter controls, including those upon the sales and distribution networks
- the establishment of a more proactive approach to selling, including the development of an internal and external sales team, the advertising campaign and the appearance at selected boat shows
- a decision on the positioning strategy that is to underpin the market effort.

The probable external problems will stem very largely from coming to terms with the very different market with which the company will be dealing and in particular the characteristics of the new customer base and competitors. Without doubt, one of the most significant issues will be concerned with the company's image, since AMC cannot afford to compromise this in the eyes of its traditional customers, but needs to capitalize upon it for its new market.

In order to overcome these problems, a number of distinct changes will be needed, the most significant and immediate of which involves overcoming the lack of marketing expertise. Perhaps the easiest and fastest way of doing this involves recruiting one or more marketing specialists to support the new marketing manager. Together, these will have responsibility for:

• market development
• the identification and development of an appropriate distribution network
• the further development and implementation of the marketing plan
• the recruitment and management of a sales team.

Other areas for action and change include:

• a formal assessment of production capability
• the development of a modified purchasing policy
• instituting a more rigorous climate of cost control
• retraining of the appropriate staff.

It is obvious from this that a considerable amount of change is needed if the company is to capitalize upon the opportunities that seemingly exist. However, without the active support of Tom Anderson and other members of the board, few changes in culture and direction will be achieved and the effort will have little real pay-off.

* * * * *

PLANNING AND CONTROL

Case 9.10: Watergate Pumps Ltd

Answer

Attention: Marketing Director, Watergate Pumps Ltd.
From: Judith Wynn, Market Analyst
Report: Recommendations for an effective environmental monetary
           system; recommendations for future marketing action.

(*a*) **An environmental monetary system**

1 Introduction and background

It is apparent from my analysis that Watergate Pumps currently has an
insufficiently detailed understanding of its external environment. The
implications of this have been highlighted by the way in which the company
has been taken by surprise by a series of market developments (for the detail
of these, refer to page 1 of the information supplied and the series of bullet
points) and by the subsequent decline in our market share (see Table 1). In
addition, we have a heavy presence in the declining local authority market
and a weak market position in the other three sectors of the market (see
Table 2). Additional evidence of our poor understanding of the market is
reflected in Table 3 (the buying motives of the different customer groups)
and our failure to reposition between 1992 and 1995.

2 The purpose and benefits of the system

The proposed system will be designed to provide the management team with
a clear and on-going picture of the market. It will focus upon a number of
areas, including:
- competitors' strengths, weaknesses, resources, strategies and performance
  levels
- customers (existing and potential) and their current and developing demands
- the general trading environment.

The benefits of the system should be seen in terms of a far clearer
understanding of the market and, in particular, of customers and competitors.
This should in turn lead to the development of far clearer, more focused and
appropriate strategic and tactical behaviour. Given this, it should then be far
less likely that the company will be taken by surprise by developments
within the market (see, for example, our failure to anticipate the entry of
Pump Suppliers in 1993, the launch of new and modified products by BG
Industrial and Northern Pumps, the general competitive repositioning, and
so on). In addition, the system should provide a basis for a more proactive
approach and a general strengthening of our competitive position.

3 The structure of the system

It is proposed that the system consists of four principal dimensions:

- Internal records
- Marketing research
- Marketing intelligence
- Marketing decision support analysis.

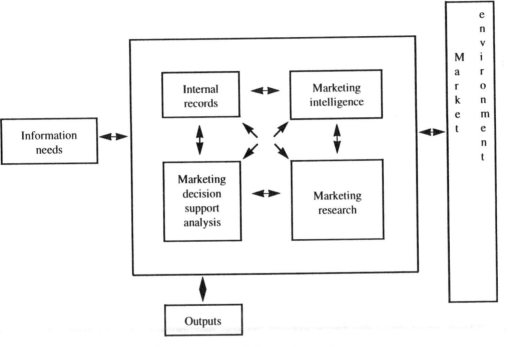

Figure 1   The information system

The relationship between these areas and the overall structure of the system are illustrated in Figure 1.

To ensure that the system is of the greatest value to the company, it will be based very firmly on an analysis of managers' information needs. It is therefore recommended that we begin by examining in detail:

- information needs
- information gaps
- the ways in which information generated by the system might best be used.

It is essential, therefore, that in developing the system we ensure that we satisfy a number of conditions, including:

- The system must be user-friendly.
- It must be manageable.
- It must provide the information that is needed for effective marketing decision making.
- It must avoid the problems of information overload.

Recognizing this, it is proposed that the system be developed and implemented over a predetermined time period. Given that the company has not had such a system in place previously, it is unrealistic to expect that the full system can be developed and introduced to the company in one move. It is therefore recommended that a timetable be established, with the system being introduced over a twelve-month period. As part of this, it is essential that the responsibility for the system is clearly allocated and that this is at a senior level in the company. The progress of the system's development will also need to be monitored.

4 The expected inputs and outputs

Although brief reference has already been made to the inputs and outputs, they can be identified more specifically as being:

Inputs

- Competitive information
- Customer information
- General market information.

These inputs will be obtained from a spectrum of sources, including the trade press, the sales force, exhibitions and distribution intermediaries. In order to collect this information, it is essential that staff are made aware of the nature of the information needed and how it will be used. It is recommended that a relatively unstructured approach is used initially (i.e. collect whatever information we can) and that this is gradually refined over time.

A fundamental part of the system is, of course, that of the analysis stage; again, it is imperative that the responsibility for analysis and dissemination is clearly allocated.

Outputs

The output from the system will take the form of a monthly report summarizing the key market developments and highlighting the apparent opportunities and threats. The monthly report will be supplemented by a weekly briefing paper.

It needs to be emphasized, however, that these reports should form the basis for subsequent marketing action, and again the responsibility for this will rest at board level. The circulation list for the reports will therefore need to be carefully determined.

5 The organizational and resource implications

The costs of the system cannot be determined at this stage. However, it needs to be recognized that the costs of *not* developing such a system are already apparent. It is therefore essential that there is a full commitment to the system – and its use – at senior management level. In terms of the immediate resource implications, it is evident that, as the newly appointed marketing analyst, I will need to spend a considerable amount of my time over the next few months developing the system. However, perhaps the most significant organizational implication can be identified in terms of the need for a far more obvious, stronger and much more consistent external focus on the part of management, with a commitment to use the outputs. Without this, the system is likely to be of little value. This can perhaps best be summarized in terms of the need for a new and much more market-oriented management culture.

6 The benefits of the system

These have been alluded to in section 3, but are in essence related to the scope for a far more proactive stance. This should be reflected most obviously in terms of:

- better market positioning
- a clearer and more focused new product development process
- better pricing
- clearer market targeting
- higher levels of customer satisfaction
- a far stronger competitive stance.

(b) Recommendations for future marketing action

1 Overview

It is apparent from my preliminary analysis that the company's market and competitive position have weakened considerably over the past few years. It is therefore essential that the current decline in market share is stopped and that the company begins targeting those parts of the market which offer significant growth opportunities (see Table 2 in the mini-case). Other issues which need to be addressed include:

- the price/perceived reliability relationship (see Figure 1(a))
- the issues of availability and perceived ease of fitting (see Figure 1(b))
- the significance of the different buying motives of each of the customer groups (see Table 3)
- the failure to make full use of the company's manufacturing capacity (see Table 1)

- the possibilities for exporting (see Table 1)
- product modification and new product development
- the quality of the products' control systems.

Underlying these points is the question of the competitive stance that the company wishes to adopt over the next few years. It is evident from the information in the case that the three principal competitors have all given greater emphasis to the issues of price, perceived reliability, ease of fitting and availability. Watergate's management needs to decide whether it will adopt a broadly similar stance or deliberately adopt a low price posture in order to achieve a degree of differentiation. There is, however, a danger in this in that evidence from the market suggests that price is not an important factor in the growing market sectors (see Table 3).

2 Recommendation

It is therefore recommended that the company increases its price, but only against the background of a series of product modifications new product actions designed to:

- improve reliability
- improve the ease of fitting
- improve the control systems.

Without these three supporting actions, the company's sales will inevitably suffer. However, taking action in these areas is unlikely to prove sufficient by itself, since the improvements will need to be communicated to the market. It is therefore recommended that a clearly focused advertising campaign be developed, with emphasis being given to these improvements. The target markets for the campaign will be the growing market sectors.

At the same time, attention needs to be paid to issues of availability (see Figure 1(b)). The information supplied provides little information on the sales and distribution approach and it is therefore difficult to make firm recommendations. It is, however, essential that a stronger, more proactive and more firmly focused approach be adopted in order to reach buyers and the appropriate decision-making units (DMUs).

Table 1 illustrates the extent to which competitors are operating in markets other than the UK and this, coupled with Watergate's failure to use its full manufacturing capacity, suggests that exporting might well be attractive. It is recommended, however, that the company views this as a medium to long-term development rather than something for the short term. The reason for this is that, until the firm has really consolidated its domestic market, it is likely to overstretch itself by moving overseas. Thought might therefore be given to how costs might be reduced and revenues increased by alternative usage of the excess capacity (one measure, of course, might be to sublet this part of the premises).

The success of the recommendations made so far will, of course, be heavily dependent upon a clear programme of implementation, and a question that must therefore be asked concerns the quality of Watergate's management. Given that the current management team has been responsible for the company's competitive decline over the past few years, reservations might possibly be expressed about issues of commitment and/or ability. However, without a far more proactive stance it is unlikely that the recommendations made here will be implemented to the extent that is needed.

* * * * *

Case 9.11 : Penton Ltd

Answer

For the attention of the main board of Penton Ltd
Part A: Recommendations for achieving identified changes

1 Management summary

1.1 Below is a summary of the key steps required:

- the appointment of a senior marketing person
- a stronger and more obvious focus for the business
- a programme of internal marketing
- a full internal and external audit;
- a stronger top-down approach, particularly in the short term
- a clarification of objectives
- a programme of market research
- a more structured planning process which incorporates a mission statement
- decisions on the competitive stance that is to be adopted
- a programme of monitoring and feedback
- increased accountability throughout the company
- a detailed assessment of new product development capability
- greater exploitation of the brand name.

2 Introduction and background

2.1 The suggestions and recommendations made here are based on our findings to date. There is, however, a need for further work with the company, particularly in the area of implementation.

2.2 The success of much of what is recommended here rests firmly on the appointment of a new senior member of the management team who will have explicit responsibility for marketing activities.

3 A marketing orientation

3.1 Penton Ltd has become overly reliant on a small number of established but ageing products. For the required change to take place, there is need for the development of a far stronger marketing orientation which will give greater explicit recognition both to the needs of the customer and to the ways in which, within a changing market, the company might gain – and retain – a significant competitive advantage. This will require a major change in corporate culture. This can best be achieved by:

- the appointment of a marketing specialist at a senior level with the responsibility for the development of a more proactive stance
- a refocusing of the business
- a programme of internal marketing so that staff are fully aware of the new direction for the company and the contributions that they will be expected to make
- an audit of current activities
- market and product development
- a programme of promotion, including public relations and advertising.

3.2 Any change of culture in these circumstances will only be achieved by a 'top-down' approach, with members of the board demonstrating their explicit commitment to customer satisfaction. The marketing and sales departments, led by the new marketing director, must therefore become the basis from which the company moves ahead.

3.3 An important part of this will be an understanding of customer and distributors' needs. There will therefore be a need for a programme of market research in order to identify:

- levels of customer satisfaction
- areas of market opportunity
- distributors' expectations
- competitors' probable moves.

3.4 A degree of refocusing will be needed so that Penton's positioning becomes more meaningful and explicit. The decision on positioning can, however, only be taken following the programme of research referred to in 3.3 above. The refocusing will be designed to achieve several objectives, but most importantly will help to clarify the company's offer.

3.5 A programme of internal marketing will then be needed in order to ensure that staff are made and kept aware of the new direction, the reasons for this, the nature of their expected contribution and the levels of success being achieved.

3.6 An audit of the current methods of operation underpins all of what has been suggested so far. This will be designed to improve levels of effectiveness and efficiency.

3.7 A programme of market and product development is needed which will reflect changing market needs and corporate capability. Assuming this is conducted effectively, the company will be able to develop and sustain a meaningful competitive advantage more effectively.

3.8 There will be the need for a programme of advertising and public relations in order to increase levels of market awareness and to support the launch of new products.

3.9 Underpinning all of this should be the development of a mission statement which encapsulates the changed values of the company (see also section 4.2).

4 A stronger and more proactive planning culture

4.1 The management philosophy has traditionally been reactive. The development of better plans and a stronger and more proactive planning culture will be designed to ensure that:
  - opportunities are more readily identified and capitalized upon
  - threats will be perceived more readily and action taken to minimize their impact
  - lead times are reduced
  - levels of effectiveness generally are increased
  - levels of accountability are increased.

4.2 This planning process should begin with the development of a mission statement which incorporates the changed values of the business. This will in turn require a series of decisions on the direction that the business is to take and the market position to be adopted.

4.3 Other areas in need of clarification are the primary and secondary corporate and functional objectives that are to be pursued.

4.4 A full environmental analysis is required.

4.5 An internal audit designed to identify the true level of corporate capability should be conducted as a matter of some urgency.

4.6 Decisions are required on a variety of areas, including:
  - the competitive stance to be adopted
  - the product development programme
  - pricing postures
  - distribution issues.

4.7 Following on from 4.6, it is essential that work begins shortly on the first drafts of the plans for all key areas, with this being led by members of the board after decisions have been made on the corporate objectives.

4.8 A programme of monitoring and feedback should be instigated, with accountability for coordination and ensuring that corrective action is taken being the specific responsibility of main board members.

4.9 Levels of accountability throughout the company need to be increased.

4.10 Given changes in all of these areas, the development of a more effective and proactive planning culture should begin to emerge. It does, however, need to be emphasized that levels of commitment to planning are only likely to increase if the plans themselves prove to be realistic rather than broad and generally unrealistic statements of intent.

5 The new product development process

5.1 The planning process referred to in section 4 must provide the rationale and direction of any changes to the new product development process. It is, however, apparent from our work so far that the R and D team currently lacks direction. It is therefore essential that the environmental analysis referred to in 4.4, and the clarification of objectives referred to in 4.3, are used as the basis of the new product development strategy.

5.2 Further work is needed on the company's true NPD capability so that a fuller assessment can be made of:

1 What NPD activity might realistically be carried out in the short and long term.

2 The particular problems currently being encountered in the process.

This can then be set against the background of the findings of the environmental analysis and, in particular, the opportunities that are likely to emerge over the next few years.

5.3 Clarification is also required of the competitive stance that the company wishes to adopt in this area, and in particular whether the company, at this stage at least, wishes to be proactive or instead intends to adopt a market follower's approach.

5.4 Given decisions in these areas, work can then be done in order to improve the various stages of new product development, including:

- market evaluation
- prototype development
- business evaluation
- text marketing.

5.5 It is essential that responsibility for NPD rests firmly at board level and is seen as part of the remit of the new marketing director (see section 3.2).

6 Summary

6.1 A series of changes have been recommended in this part of the report. We have deliberately not put costings next to them, since these will be the focus of subsequent work. However, for our suggestions to be worthwhile, it is essential that levels of accountability are increased and stronger direction is given from the top.

Part B: Implications for approaches to management control

7 Overview

The implications for management control of our recommendations are significant and can be seen in terms of the need for changes both in attitudes and operating practice.

7.1 Changes in attitude

With regard to attitudes, the key issue is the need for management to recognize that previous approaches to planning and control have been unsatisfactory and that this is due largely to failings in areas such as:

- the setting of objectives
- the implementation of plans

- feedback and follow-up mechanisms.

The attitudinal change required is therefore concerned with recognition of the current inadequacies and a willingness to adopt a more structured and demanding approach to management. Included within this is the willingness to accept the discipline of regular and detailed market analysis and the establishment and implementation of more firmly structured plans throughout the business.

7.2 Changes in operating practice

This attitudinal shift can be seen to overlap with the second dimension referred to above, that of changes in operating practice. If the recommendations made in the report that forms the answer to (a) are to be implemented, there is therefore the need for a fully integrated planning and control process, since the control dimension is meaningless if the planning dimension has not been properly developed. Thus, as we observed above, there is a need for:

- a clear statement of objectives
- a clear statement of the competitive stance;
- a firm positioning statement with an attendant clarification of the target markets
- an unambiguous and realistic plan which covers both the corporate and the departmental activities
- a firm allocation of responsibilities and structured delegation
- a clarification of timescales
- a programme of staff training
- an improvement in communication patterns
- a more collaborative ethos.

Underlying this is a far more definitive statement of accountability.

8 Summary

The specifics of the control process follow logically from this, and centre around the establishment of intermediate objectives and the development of feedback and control mechanisms. In this way performances can be compared with targets and, where appropriate, corrective action taken.

Against this background, it can be seen that in many ways the implications of our earlier suggestions for the control process are relatively straightforward, and can best be summarized in terms of a far stronger process of monitoring, feedback, accountability and corrective action. With regard to specific activities, these include:

- regular customer surveys
- trade surveys
- competitive monitoring
- performance monitoring of both financial and marketing measures
- performance against plan.

★　★　★　★　★

PLANNING AND CONTROL

Case 9.12: New Directions plc

Answer

To: Main board of directors, New Directions plc
From: G. Richards, Senior Consultant, Marketing Update plc
Subject: Strategic marketing at New Directions plc
Date: 15 December 1995

Background

Following our appointment as marketing consultants to New Directions plc with a view to improving the competitive position of the company, I am pleased to be able to offer this preliminary report for your attention. The report is divided into two key areas.

The first part of the report comprises two SWOT analyses, one covering the period before the takeover by the group and one covering the period post-takeover up to the current time. It was decided, after preliminary discussions, that this 'pre'-and 'post'-takeover SWOT approach would be useful in understanding the decline in New Directions' competitive position. Based on the insights which these analyses have provided, the first part of the report also outlines the implications of the post-takeover SWOT analysis for methods of marketing planning and control.

Part 2 of the report builds on the strategic review in Part 1 to develop recommended courses of action in order for New Directions to improve its market standing and competitive position.

1 Pre- and post-takeover SWOT analyses and implications for methods of marketing planning and control

1.1 Pre-takeover SWOT analysis

Note: This analysis is based on the period covering 1987–1990, i.e. the period immediately preceding takeover by the group. At this time the managing director of New Directions was Thomas Oakley, who had led the company for some ten years.

Strengths

- An entrepreneurial and aggressive management style (due largely to the approach of Thomas Oakley)
- A young, enthusiastic and highly motivated management team
- A strong market presence with 400 stores and expanding

- Clear positioning and a major player in the 15–25, C1/C2, male and female fashion sectors
- Reputation in City as an ambitious, design-led company with strong growth record.
- Market-customer-led.

Weaknesses

- Some evidence of lack of strong/forward control procedures, especially financial
- Image in City of unconventional, sometimes maverick, approach
- Inexperienced management team.

Opportunities

- Growth of European market; increase in intra-European trade; Spanish market, in particular, attractive
- UK fashion market still growing
- Early signs of growth in both children's market for fashion clothing and in 30–40-year-old group.

Threats

- UK/European retailing becoming extremely competitive
- Signs of decline in current market segment of New Directions
- Move in market towards higher quality.

1.2 Post-takeover SWOT analysis

Note: This analysis is based on an investigation into the current (1995) situation at New Directions.

Strengths

- Recognition of need for stronger financial controls
- Access to group financial resources
- More conventional image in City.

Weaknesses

- Financial rather than marketing orientation
- Lack of retailing experience among current managerial staff
- Risk-aversive, lack of entrepreneurial skills
- Unclear/confused image in marketplace
- Too much emphasis on price at expense of quality
- Poor staff morale.

Opportunities

- Still fast growth in European, and especially Spanish, markets
- 30–40-year-olds sector in UK now forecast to grow at 12 per cent per annum
- Growth in fashion market for children's clothing now confirmed
- Customers looking for 'exciting shopping experiences': possibilities for new retail concepts.

Threats

- Competitors more aware of market trends and moves towards new retail concepts
- Possibilities in Europe largely ignored
- Market share decreasing
- Greater proportion of customers looking for quality rather than low prices.

1.3 Implications of post-takeover SWOT analysis for methods of marketing planning and control

Overall, the post-takeover SWOT analysis confirms that over recent years the competitive market position has worsened considerably and the company is in a much weaker position. It is difficult to conclude anything other than that this worsened position is largely due to the loss of the entrepreneurial and marketing skills of the previous managing director, Thomas Oakley, followed, more recently, by many of the younger staff trained during Mr Oakley's time. Part 2 of this report contains recommended courses of action to improve the competitive position of New Directions, which will be considered shortly. However, the post-takeover SWOT analysis also suggests a number of general implications for methods of marketing planning and control at New Directions as follows.

(a) Marketing orientation/marketet analysis

Effective marketing planning stems from a marketing rather than financial orientation and, as such, needs to be based on detailed and up-to-date market analysis. This does not mean that financial control and performance are unimportant, but financial performance itself is determined by how market-oriented a company is. There is a lack of marketing orientation at New Directions due to an over-emphasis on financial controls. In addition, and related to this, there is a lack of market analysis, leading to lost opportunities and a lack of awareness of threats. Now that the previous managing director, Thomas Oakley, has gone, his 'feel' for the marketplace needs to be replaced by an effective system of market research and intelligence gathering.

(b) The importance of clear marketing objectives and strategies

Again, since the departure of Oakley with his entrepreneurial approach, New Directions lacks a systematic approach to identifying and selecting marketing objectives and strategies. This has led to a lack of strategic direction and confused positioning in the market. Specific and measurable marketing objectives need to be established, together with both short- and long-term marketing strategies.

(c) Adequate staff training and motivation

Marketing plans count for nothing unless and until they are translated into action. This, in turn, requires that staff are adequately trained and motivated.

As the SWOT analysis shows, currently staff lack both training and motivation.

2 Action recommendations based on strategic review

2.1 Introduction

Based on the findings from the SWOT analysis outlined in Part 1, we have pleasure in suggesting the following recommendations for future marketing at New Directions.

2.2 Identification of alternatives

Although several variations can be identified, broadly the following represent the major alternatives for New Directions:

1 Do nothing
2 Consolidate and wait for an economic upturn.
3 Radical surgery.

Alternative (1) is not recommended. Of the three alternatives, this is the most dangerous. Market share and sales are both falling rapidly. In addition, the market is also changing rapidly. Doing nothing will lead to further losses in sales and market share. Alternative (2), although slightly less dangerous, is in fact also not recommended. Although the market is currently in flux and demand depressed, the most effective way to deal with these factors is positive action.

2.3 Recommended alternative/action plans

Alternative 3, therefore, is the alternative suggested. As the SWOT analysis shows, New Directions is now badly out of touch with the marketplace and has a confused positioning strategy/image. In addition, the company is failing to react to major opportunities and threats. Only radical changes will deal with these problems. Specifically, the actions recommended are as follows.

Immediate actions
- Appointment of a new marketing director, preferably with experience in fashion retailing.
- Introduction of staff training, plus appointment of more experienced staff.
- A recognition of the need for a more marketing-oriented approach.
- Development of Spanish market to be put on hold.

Medium term (3–6 months)
- Detailed analysis of market trends and changes, including major demographic, economic and competitive trends. On-going market research and information system to be established.
- Identification and selection of specific marketing objectives and strategies

to include selection of target markets and repositioning strategies. These are likely to include catering for the growth 30–40-year-old segment and, in the longer run, developing new outlets catering for the children's fashion market.
- Based on the above, a start should be made on developing new retailing concepts to include carefully planned and interpreted plans for merchandising policies, including product ranges, quality, prices and store refurbishment.
- Detailed analysis of European market to be commenced.

Longer term (6–18 months)
- Definitive plans and programmes for new retailing concepts (see earlier) to be developed.
- Plans for developing export markets in Europe to be initiated.
- Plans for expansion/opening of new outlets to be developed.

We look forward to discussing the contents of this report in more detail at our next meeting in September.

★　★　★　★　★

Appendix: a synopsis of past Advanced Certificate and Diploma mini-case questions for The Chartered Institute of Marketing examinations from Syllabus 94

This appendix has been included for your information. It covers Promotional Practice and Management Information for Marketing and Sales – the two common Advanced Certificate subjects – plus Effective Management for Sales and Sales Operations from the Advanced Certificate in Sales Management paper, in addition to Effective Management for Marketing and Marketing Operations from the Advanced Certificate in Marketing paper. At Diploma level it covers questions from International Marketing Strategy, Marketing Communications Strategy and the Planning and Control paper of the two subjects that form Strategic Marketing Management (the other subject, Analysis and Decision, is the maxi-case study and questions are not reproduced here as it would be inappropriate within the context of this book). In each example, the first set of questions under that subject relates to the December 1994 sitting and the second set to the June 1995 sitting.

This section has been deliberately put in as an appendix as it is merely meant to serve as an information resource and to give you a feel for the variety and style of questions that are asked in relation to mini-cases from Syllabus 94 papers. It is not meant to serve any instructional purposes.

The main point that should be remembered is that all of these sets of examination questions carry 50 per cent of the total of the marks for each of the papers that have been noted. It goes without saying that the importance of the mini-case within the examination cannot be too strongly emphasized.

Promotional Practice

Example 1

As the account manager of one of the chosen agencies you are required to write proposals in an outline report for the opening of the new TGI Friday's. In particular your report should include the following:

(a) Recommendations on the selection of different types of above-the-line media and their scheduling. **(20 marks)** (*b*) Guidelines on how public relations activities can be used to support the above-the-line media campaign. **(10 marks)**

(*c*) The benefits and operation of using a database in order to retain customers. **(10 marks)**

(*d*) Recommendations on the allocation of the £100k budget. **(10 marks)**

Example 2

As the advertising controller at Adams you are required by your marketing director to write proposals in an outline report for the launch of the Adams chain in Spain. Your report should cover the following issues:

(*a*) The identification of promotional objectives for the launch campaign. **(15 marks)**

(*b*) Your initial recommendations regarding the Intermedia selection and scheduling for the launch of Adams within Spain given a budget of the equivalent of £1M for the six-month campaign. You can assume that Spanish media costs and availability are similar to those within the UK. **(20 marks)**

(*c*) The merits and disadvantages of appointing a Spanish advertising agency to handle the launch campaign rather than to utilize the UK agency. **(15 marks)**

Management Information for Marketing and Sales

Example 3

You have been appointed to manage the Marketing Information System to establish information systems that will enable the company to take advantage of new opportunities as they arise. Given the background information to the case including relevant tables you are required to write a report to the Directors to evaluate the current situation and to produce an action plan for discussion at the next meeting of the management team of EPS Ltd.

(*a*) Your report should identify problem areas and explain the importance of the issues raised. **(15 marks)**

(*b*) Your report should suggest possible solutions to the problems identified including in your analysis appropriate calculations in support of your recommendations. **(20 marks)**

(*c*) Finally, you should be able to suggest further information that should be obtained to help manage the business more effectively. **(15 marks)**

Example 4

Prepare a report for Dr R. Jones, the Chairman of the management committee for the theatre, addressing the following matters:

(a) What further information might be needed to help managers plan and assess business performance during the next budget period. **(20 marks)**

(b) What the effect of increasing capacity from 60 per cent to 75 per cent would achieve in the next budget period in terms of income, expenditure and profit. You should prepare a revised flexible budget in support of your answer. **(20 marks)**

(c) Suggestions as to how technology might be used as a key tool in providing information to assist managers in implementing their stated objectives. **(10 marks)**

Effective Management for Sales

Example 5

(a) Advise David Warren on how he might reorganize his sales force assuming that he persuades the better salespeople to relocate.
(25 marks)

(b) Assuming an alternative scenario where most of the more productive sales staff decide to leave rather than relocate, advise David how he can recruit and select replacements. **(25 marks)**

Example 6

(a) Advise Malcolm on a training programme he could institute for the new salespeople. **(25 marks)**

(b) How should Geoff approach the problem of rewards to the whole sales force? **(25 marks)**

Sales Operations

Example 7

Assume the role of Tony Mallett and prepare a report for Caroline McArthy. The report should be in two parts:

(a) Calculate the number of salespeople required and suggest an appropriate organization of the sales force for the region. Also outline your suggested method of journey planning for the new sales representatives.
(25 marks)

(b) What functions and role do you recommend that the new office should provide? **(25 marks)**

Example 8

Assume the role of Jenny Buchanan and prepare a report for the forthcoming meeting which:

(a) Details the type of information required for the sales information and record system and how it could be obtained. **(25 marks)**

(b) Provides examples of the analysis and evaluation measures that could be used in the management of a sales force. **(25 marks)**

Effective Management for Marketing

Example 9

Prepare a plan for presentation to the Governors indicating the following:

(a) The actions you propose to take to audit the extent of the resources, particularly the volunteers' skills available within the Foundation. Clearly indicate to the Governors how you would implement these and over what time frame. **(20 marks)**

(b) Outline your proposals for managing the necessary programme of change to reorganize the Foundation to ensure a centrally coordinated and supported programme of activities. **(20 marks)**

(c) Indicate clearly how you would recommend presenting these changes to the volunteers to avoid losing their support and to ensure their continued motivation and the maintenance of the local impetus. **(10 marks)**

Example 10

(a) What factors have led to the reduction in management numbers described in this article and what are the implications of these changes for the motivation and development of tomorrow's generation of managers? **(15 marks)**

(b) The table indicates a wide variation of redundancy levels between the companies. How would you explain these differences? **(10 marks)**

(c) Bearing in mind the changing nature of the management role generally, what would be the characteristics and aptitudes you would look for when selecting a marketing management trainee? Explain these in the context of the role and responsibilities you would expect this manager to take on in the future. **(15 marks)**

(d) What recommendations would you make for the development of a suitable two-year development programme for such a trainee?
(10 marks)

Marketing Operations

Example 11

In the role of a marketing advisor, write a business report covering the following aspects:

(a) The case suggests that opportunities are likely to arise for crossovers or joint ventures with other forms of home entertainment. Assume that Nintendo is considering liaising with partners from the electronics industry and music business to develop an integrated home entertainment system. Nintendo decides to conduct a marketing audit to provide input into the marketing planning process. Explain the categories of information which should be collected. **(25 marks)**

(b) What legal, regulatory, ethical or social responsibility constraints might Nintendo have to consider before making marketing decisions?

(15 marks)

(c) What do you think are the main opportunities arising from the cooperative deals in which Nintendo might become involved? **(10 marks)**

Example 12

As a consultant assisting Ben & Jerry's draft a report which covers the following:

(a) Ben & Jerry's adopts a proactive stance on social responsibility issues. Describe the types of social responsibility issues in which the company might become involved and explain the benefits which this involvement might offer. **(15 marks)**

(b) Give an explanation of the reasons why marketing planning could help Ben & Jerry's become established in an overseas market such as the UK. **(10 marks)**

(c) Describe the areas which a detailed marketing plan for Ben & Jerry's should cover. **(25 marks)**

International Marketing Strategy

Example 13

(a) What are the main strategic options available to WFS in international markets? Examine how you could use country attractiveness/competitive strength and other analytical techniques to improve WFS's international marketing strategy. **(25 marks)**

(b) Examine the particular difficulties that WFS would be likely to experience in implementing its international marketing plans. **(25 marks)**

Example 14

(a) Wishing to expand into international markets Pivovar have retained your services as an international marketing consultant. Taking full account of the information in the case, write a brief report examining the different ways in which Pivovar might expand its sales revenues and profits from international markets together with the implications for each choice. **(25 marks)**

(b) Pivovar have been approached by a major player in the global beer market with a view of acquiring the company. In the event of the takeover succeeding, what advice would you give the new owners in marketing the Pivovar brand globally. **(25 marks)**

Marketing Communications Strategy

Example 15

In your role as the newly appointed Marketing Communications Manager of Mercury One-2-One, you are asked to write a report to Mr Goswell, managing director, covering the marketing communications strategy and plan for 1995.
The plan should specifically contain:

* A definition of the target markets in the UK.
* The problems which marketing communications can help solve and the messages to be used to achieve the company's strategy.
* Promotion methods recommended for the business market and the consumer market.
* A timetable of promotional activities for 1995. **(50 marks)**

Example 16

You have recently joined the team responsible for marketing the hotel complex to both consumer and business markets. You are now asked to write an outline report recommending a marketing communications strategy for the next two years (1996 and 1997). In your report you are specifically asked to include:

* A business mission for the hotel and marketing objectives.
* Definitions of domestic and international target markets.
* Promotional methods for consumer and business markets.
* A budget and a timetable of promotional activities.
* Mechanisms for integrating the whole promotional strategy. **(50 marks)**

Planning and Control

Example 17

(a) Using a model of your choice, comment upon the apparent state of the firm's portfolio. In doing this, you should specify any assumptions that you make, the limitations of the model and any other information that you would require before recommending how the firm's portfolio should be developed. You should also identify briefly any other approach to portfolio analysis that might be used to evaluate the portfolio. **(25 marks)**

(b) In the light of the research findings, prepare a report for the managing director identifying the key dimensions of a customer care programme and how such a programme might be introduced to the organization. In doing this, you should pay particular attention to issues of implementation. **(25 marks)**

Example 18

(a) Prepare a report for the managing director identifying the criteria by which the three recommendations might best be evaluated. **(15 marks)**

(b) Prepare an outline marketing plan for the launch of a new holiday destination. In doing this you should make detailed reference to the sort of financial and non-financial information that would be needed to underpin the plan.   **(35 marks)**

Index

Please note that this index has been compiled within the context of examination technique plus a listing (*in italics*) of individual case studies and case study answers. It does not include technical aspects of marketing which arise in individual cases and solutions, as this would be inappropriate in this particular context. It is expected that such technical aspects of marketing will already be known from a study of marketing principles through appropriate literature or programmes of study.

THIRD EDITION

Marketing PLANS

HOW TO PREPARE THEM: HOW TO USE THEM

MALCOLM McDONALD

- The UK's top marketing bestseller

- Written by the UK's top marketing guru

- Greatly expanded to include recent developments in marketing techniques

- Combines theory with practice

- Practical step-by-step guide

- Ideal for marketing managers and business executives

- Recommended reading for the CIM examinations

- Resource pack available for tutors

To Order:
Phone: 01933 414000

March 1995 • 246 x 189mm • 360pp
Paperback • 0 7506 2213 X

BUTTERWORTH
HEINEMANN